Advance praise for *God's on the Phone*

"Regis Flaherty makes you want to be a better person, a better child of God. With humor, wit, and humility, he shows how life is a journey full of possibilities for learning and redemption."

—Joyce Duriga, editor, *Catholic New World,*
the newspaper for the Archdiocese of Chicago

"For heaven's sake, don't hang up! Read this book and experience God's presence in the ordinary rhythm of daily life—and appreciate the choices each of us has in cooperating with his grace. Take this call!"

—Kerry Crawford, author of *Lourdes Today:*
A Pilgrimage to Mary's Grotto

"In this delightful book, Regis Flaherty shares the power of God's grace in the lives of everyday people. Flaherty is a master storyteller whose personal holiness shines through as an inspiration to any reader."

—Mike Sullivan, president of Catholics United for the Faith
and publisher of Emmaus Road Publishing

"Regis Flaherty has provided a heartwarming treasury of inspirational stories and meditative reflections from the Bible, the Catechism, our popes, and saints of the Church. Reading this book makes me want to perform the works of mercy more consistently in my own life."

—Laurie Manhardt, PH.D., creator of *Come and See:*
Catholic Bible Study

GOD'S ON THE PHONE

God's on the Phone

STORIES OF GRACE IN ACTION

REGIS J. FLAHERTY

SERVANT
BOOKS

PUBLISHED BY ST. ANTHONY MESSENGER PRESS
CINCINNATI, OHIO

The Nihil obstat and the imprimatur are declarations that this work is considered to be free from doctrinal or moral error. It is not implied that those who have granted the same agree with the contents, opinions, or statements expressed. Givin this thirtieth day of September, two thousand ten.

David Allen Zubik
Bishop of Pittsburgh

Unless otherwise noted, Scripture passages have been taken from the *Revised Standard Version*, Catholic edition. Copyright 1946, 1952, 1971 by the Division of Christian Education of the National Council of Churches of Christ in the USA. Used by permission. All rights reserved. Some Scripture texts in this work (indicated by *NAB*) are taken from the *New American Bible with Revised New Testament and Revised Psalms* © 1991, 1986, 1970 Confraternity of Christian Doctrine, Washington, D.C., and are used by permission of the copyright owner. All rights reserved. Quotations taken from the English translation of the *Catechism of the Catholic Church* for the United States of America (indicated as *CCC*), 2nd ed., copyright 1997 by United States Catholic Conference–Libreria Editrice Vaticana are used by permission.

Cover and book design by Mark Sullivan
Cover image ©Ocean Photography | Veer

LIBRARY OF CONGRESS CATALOGING-IN-PUBLICATION DATA
Flaherty, Regis J.
God's on the phone : stories of grace in action / Regis Flaherty.
p. cm.
Includes bibliographical references.
ISBN 978-0-86716-978-2 (alk. paper)
1. Spiritual life–Christianity. 2. Christian life. I. Title. II. Title: God is on the phone.
III. Title: Stories of grace in action.
BV4501.3.F5773 2011
248.4–dc23
2011021084

ISBN: 978-0-86716-978-2

Copyright ©2011, Regis J. Flaherty. All rights reserved.

Published by Servant Books, an imprint of
St. Anthony Messenger Press.
28 W. Liberty St.
Cincinnati, OH 45202
www.AmericanCatholic.org
www.Servantbooks.org

Printed in the United States of America.
Printed on acid-free paper.
11 12 13 14 15   1 2 3 4 5

I am well aware that I have inherited the spiritual blessings of great men and women—that I am the descendant of righteous people who loved God, showed mercy, and kept covenant. I dedicate this book to them, especially to my parents and grandparents, who by their faithfulness to God gave me so much. By God's grace may I also pass that blessing to my children and grandchildren.

These were men of mercy,
  whose righteous deeds have not been forgotten;
their prosperity will remain with their descendants,
  and their inheritance to their children's children.

—Sirach 44:10‑11

I, the LORD, your God…[bestow] mercy down to the thousandth generation, on the children of those who love me and keep my commandments.

—Exodus 20:5‑6, *NAB*

ACKNOWLEDGMENTS

I thank Angie DeWitt; Richard Grebenc; Sr. Mary Francine Horos, CSSF; and Cindy Russman, who read the first draft of the manuscript and gave valuable input to improve the text. I also thank Cindy Cavnar of Servant Books for all of her work in bringing this book to publication. I especially thank my wife, Libbie, for her help in editing the text and for all her support and patience.

God is the Great Catechist. He works with us individually, teaching each person in the manner in which he or she is most likely to learn. Elijah heard God best in a whisper (see 1 Kings 19:11–13). God taught the apostles an important lesson when their boat was ready to capsize in a storm: Their fear drove them to seek the Lord, and he saved them (Matthew 8:23–26). St. Joseph found God's will when angels spoke to him in dreams (Matthew 1:19–21; 2:13). St. Paul literally needed to be knocked to the ground and temporarily blinded before he was able to see the truth about Christ (Acts 9:3–6).

I'm definitely not an Elijah. The subtle often escapes me. During my life God has regularly needed to shout to get my attention. And my learning style is by association. I understand best when I see the bigger picture through events that happen in my life or through stories that I have read or been told. In this the glory and thanks belong to God, for he has taught me in the way in which I am best able to learn. If he had dealt with me as he dealt with Elijah, I think I'd be in a heap of spiritual trouble today!

So I've had much of my spiritual education through events and stories. This book contains narratives of some of them. None are apocryphal tales. I have been personally involved in some, witnessed others, and received firsthand reports of the others from credible witnesses.

Among these thirty stories there are three that are my reflective retellings of passages from Scripture. The Bible is not all didactic. In fact, the Pontifical Biblical Commission has taught that the lessons of Scripture are often communicated through "the form of story and personal testimony."

> The Old Testament in fact presents a *story* of salvation, the powerful recital of which provides the substance of the profession of faith, liturgy, and catechesis (see Psalm 78:3–4; Exodus 12:24–27; Deuteronomy 6:20–25; 26:5–11). For its own part, the proclamation of the Christian kerygma amounts in essentials to a sequence *telling the story* of the life, death and resurrection of Jesus Christ, events of which the gospels offer us a detailed account.[1]

In other words, much of Scripture tells the story of faith as manifested in the people who lived it. By reflecting on that narrative— those stories—with the help of the Church and the light of the Holy Spirit, we can see God's divine plan of salvation.

Each of the thirty chapters herein can stand alone. I've placed a brief description of the topic with each title so you can easily choose one that interests you. Every chapter contains five elements. I tell a story, from which I draw a moral or lesson. Then I provide a quote from Scripture and another from the *Catechism of the Catholic Church* or other Catholic document or spiritual writing, grounding the lesson within the teaching of the Church. Each chapter ends with a prayer and questions for personal reflection or group discussion.

I share these stories with the hope and the prayer that they will bless you. In fact, that is also part of the plan of the Supreme Catechist and Teacher. He wants us to learn from each other. He wants us to be channels of grace to those around us.

I hope that my tales will prompt you to reflect on how God has worked in your life—your personal story, your testimony. I also pray that I, the writer, and you, the reader, would be challenged to cooperate with God in writing the remaining stories of our lives. It is in that spirit that I offer these essays to you.

Can You Give Me a Witness?
::: On preaching by example :::

My maternal grandfather, Frederick R. Wolf, was born on May 24, 1891, to Frederick and Emma Dorn Wolf. Fred was the oldest of seven children. His mother died during a flu epidemic while her children were still young.

Fred left school after sixth grade to begin work. He later took business courses at Duffs Iron City College in Pittsburgh. He learned to type, and he learned accounting, two skills that would eventually keep him employed while raising a family.

One skill that he did not obtain was the ability to drive a car. Fred walked or took a bus or a trolley to reach destinations near and far. I wonder if this inability to drive was part of his character formation. My grandfather was never in a hurry. He always paced himself. He always had time to talk and visit with people. Perhaps the waiting for public transportation was training in the virtue of patience, which he possessed in spades. Or perhaps he didn't bother to learn to drive because he loved the social interaction that was available while waiting for or riding the trolley.

My father was the biggest male influence in my life, but Pap Wolf was certainly the second most important influence. Pap's personality was a balance to my father's approach to life. My dad was task-oriented; my grandfather was relational. My father had only a few friends, while my grandfather seemed to know everyone and consider everyone a friend or a potential friend. For my father a walk was a means to get to a destination to fulfill a responsibility or complete a task. For my grandfather a walk was for the joy of walking, meeting people, and talking. A stroll down the street was an adventure. Whom would he meet? To whom would he talk, and what stories would they share?

Even the destination was often in doubt. Certainly the route could vary widely. It was not the destination that mattered to my grandfather; it was the adventure of the journey.

I will be forever thankful for the work ethic and sense of responsibility that were instilled in me by my father. But I would be lost without the love for people that I gained from my Grandfather Wolf. He treated every person, no matter his or her state in life, with respect and deference. People smiled when they saw him.

His regular walks took him to the barbershop, the bakery, and the drugstore. I loved to walk with him. At the drugstore he would buy me a cherry Coke. The treat was wonderful, but it was what I learned on our walks that left a lasting impression.

Grandfather was a creature of habit—good habits. He never passed a Catholic church without stopping for a visit to Our Lord in the tabernacle. Every morning he attended Mass. Our family would tease him because he knew so many prisoners. The reason was that often he'd attend Mass at the jail and talk with the incarcerated.

Grandfather worked tirelessly for the St. Vincent de Paul Society. Sometimes he would let me help him. We'd empty the poor box at church and deposit the money in the bank. Sometimes we'd drop in on a needy family, and he would leave them with scrips for food at a local grocer. He'd chat with the family. *Was there anything they needed? The kids looked well. There might be a job opening at the mill.* When we left he would thank them for allowing us to visit.

He would take public transportation to Catholic churches all over the city in order to be a pallbearer for indigent people. He had a pair of white gloves that he reserved for those occasions. It was obvious to me, even at a young age, that he considered it an honor to carry the casket of someone who had died penniless.

My grandfather loved his children and grandchildren. He would take two buses to come to our home each Friday to give my mother some assistance and spend time with his grandchildren. He would stop on the way and buy rolls and fresh bread at the bakery—a great treat for all of us. He would regularly slip my mother a few dollars, so that she would have some extra money in her tight budget. He would often give each of the children a quarter—a treasure in our eyes.

When I was scheduled to take my entrance exam for the pre-seminary high school program, it was he who took me on two buses and waited patiently while I took the lengthy test. He met me afterward and introduced me to another first—a visit to a bar. He had a beer and I a coke to go with our greasy burgers. It was part of the passage of growing up. Our relationship was at a new level, no longer merely that of a man and a child. We were two men together.

Throughout high school Grandfather's impact on my life continued. He sincerely wanted to know of my progress. His encouragement was important as I struggled with academics, athletics, and relationships. Tough teen years were made a little more bearable because my grandfather was there.

He came to my high school graduation. I received an award at that event for the "student who above and beyond his pursuit of academic excellence had distinguished himself by his dedication, generosity, and service." My grandfather was the first to grab my hand afterward and congratulate me. I thanked him, but I told him that it was not the most important award. "Pap, the award for the best student academically was the highest award."

Perhaps for the first time he corrected me. "No, Rege, the most important honor is for the one who serves generously. You received the most important reward." There were tears in his eyes and in mine as well.

Not many months later an administrator at my college dorm called me to the telephone. The call was to inform me that my grandfather had died. He had had a heart attack, fittingly enough while out on one of his many excursions. I cried freely, for I knew that a great man had died.

He was not ostentatious. Today I can't quote many words that he spoke. But I know what his hand felt like on my shoulder. In my mind's eye I still can see him drop to one knee as the church bell rang for the Angelus. I still can see him remove his hat as he passed an outdoor shrine to the Blessed Mother. He never preached to me, but in a real sense, his entire life was an elegant sermon.

Points to Ponder

> I assure you, my sons, that when a Christian carries out with love the most insignificant everyday action, that action overflows with the transcendence of God.... The Christian vocation consists in making heroic verse out of the prose of each day. Heaven and earth seem to merge, my sons, on the horizon. But where they really meet is in your hearts, when you sanctify your everyday lives.[1]
>
> —St. Josemaría Escrivá, *Conversations*

4

Modern man listens more willingly to witnesses than to teachers, and if he does listen to teachers, it is because they are witnesses. [2]

—Pope Paul VI, *Evangelii Nuntiandi*, no. 41

Remember the Lord our God all your days, my son, and refuse to sin or to transgress his commandments. Live uprightly all the days of your life, and do not walk in the ways of wrongdoing....

...Do not hold over till the next day the wages of any man who works for you, but pay him at once; and if you serve God you will receive payment.

Watch yourself, my son, in everything you do, and be disciplined in all your conduct. And what you hate, do not do to any one.... Give of your bread to the hungry, and of your clothing to the naked. Give all your surplus to charity, and do not let your eye begrudge the gift when you make it. Place your bread on the grave of the righteous.... Seek advice from every wise man, and do not despise any useful counsel. Bless the Lord God on every occasion; ask him that your ways may be made straight and that all your paths and plans may prosper.

—Tobit 4:5, 14–15, 16–17, 18–19

Prayer

Thank you, heavenly Father, for all of the people I have met who, by their example, have shown me what it means to live a holy life. Bless them for their faithfulness to you.

Father, as I have been blessed, I desire to bless others. Help me to live my life with commitment and obedience to you. I realize that it is only to the degree that I am faithful to you that I will be able to touch others and lead them to you. I ask this through my Lord and your Son, Jesus Christ, in union with the Holy Spirit. Amen.

Discussion Questions and Action Steps

1. Of the people you have known, who was the most influential Christian witness? Why?

2. Who in your life looks to you as an example? Describe how you have been a good witness to that person.

3. The Church puts before us the saints as examples. Do you have a favorite saint, and if so, how is he or she an example to you? Ask for that saint's intercession.

Embracing Obedience

::: On obedience :::

I had the great blessing of knowing the Most Reverend Vincent Leonard (1908–1994), the ninth bishop of the diocese of Pittsburgh. As I was discerning the priesthood in high school and college, I had several conversations with him. He was always gracious, helpful, and encouraging.

When I decided to leave the seminary at midterm of my sophomore year in college, Bishop Leonard asked if I would come to his office so that we could talk. He asked about my well-being and my family. Then, after chatting for a while, he came to the question that had prompted the meeting. "Rege," he said, "I'm told that you're leaving the seminary, and I'm wondering why. Would you mind telling me your reasons?"

I responded, "Bishop, as I've been praying, I feel God is calling me to something else."

I was a bit surprised when he stopped me. "Rege, that's all I need to know."

As our conversation continued, he told me that his door was always open for me. He gave me some spiritual counsel, but his primary concern had been addressed. He was satisfied to know that I was leaving the seminary in obedience to a call from God.

Years later I was the assistant director of the Catholic Cemeteries of the Diocese of Pittsburgh, and Bishop Leonard was elderly and long retired. The cemetery association had refurbished an elegant old stone building with burial crypts as the future place for entombment of diocesan bishops. When the building was completed, there was a service to consecrate it as "Shepherd's Rest Mausoleum." All the living bishops, active and retired, were on hand for the dedication, including Bishop Leonard.

After the dedication service he grabbed me by the arm and pulled me aside. With a smile and a twinkle in his eye, he said, "Rege, you and I are Irish. You know I belong in the ground and not in some fancy mausoleum, but when you're the bishop, you do what they tell you." He was the first to be buried in those crypts.

Obedience was important to Bishop Leonard—obedience to God, as was shown in the conversation when I left the seminary, and obedience to those in authority, even when they were his juniors. Obedience is one of the theological virtues, along with poverty and chastity—the three vows or promises taken by consecrated religious men and women. Yet these three virtues are not meant only for them. The *Catechism of the Catholic Church* teaches that poverty, chastity, and obedience are requirements for all Catholics (see *CCC*, #915)—although how each person lives these counsels varies with the person's state of life (married, single, priest, or consecrated religious).

Obedience is a bending of the will to the authority of another. Its synonyms include *submission* and *docility*.

Most people will agree that obedience is an important virtue in children. Certainly many children have been spared a scalded hand because they obeyed their mother and didn't touch the hot stove. Good grades and a good college are often the result of obedience to teachers and parents who expected dedicated studies. Yes, obedience in children is generally viewed as a good thing. However, what about adults?

Unfortunately, obedience in an adult is too often viewed as a sign of weakness and lack of freedom. However, it is neither. Obedience is a virtue of the strong. To entrust self to God and his plan requires inner strength. Rather than being enslaved to sin and selfishness, the obedient man finds a freedom to do good when he walks in the plan of God. Bishop Leonard truly illustrated this truth.

Obedience to God is also a means of praising him. Certainly free will is the greatest gift bestowed upon us by the Creator. To freely give up my will and submit to God or to those he has placed over me is, therefore, a great offering to God. Jesus made the connection explicit when he commanded the devil in the desert, "Begone, Satan! for it is written, 'You shall worship the Lord your God and him only shall you serve' " (Matthew 4:10). To obey—serve God—is to worship.

Jesus is the most excellent model of obedience. He said that he came to do the will of his heavenly Father. The disobedience of Adam and Eve had introduced sin into the lives of men. Christ's obedience set us free from the power of sin and Satan while opening the gates of heaven. In the Garden of Gethsemane, Jesus prayed that he might be spared the crucifixion, but he wanted nothing less than the full will of his Father. In obedience to his Father, he took up the cross, with all the pain and rejection that accompanied it.

Jesus was also obedient to earthly authority. He followed the rules and regulations of Judaism and was obedient to his parents (see Luke 2:51). We too are to obey lawful authority, unless it is at variance with the commands of God.

Points to Ponder

[Jesus] replied, "Rather, blessed are those who hear the word of God and observe it."

—Luke 11:28, *NAB*

Slaves, be obedient to those who are your earthly masters, with fear and trembling, in singleness of heart, as to Christ; not in the way of eye-service, as men-pleasers, but as servants of Christ, doing the will of God from the heart, rendering service with a good will as to the Lord and not to men.

—Ephesians 6:5–7

The laity should, as all Christians, promptly accept in Christian obedience decisions of their spiritual shepherds, since they are representatives of Christ as well as teachers and rulers in the Church. Let them follow the example of Christ, who by His obedience even unto death, opened to all men the blessed way of the liberty of the children of God. Nor should they omit to pray for those placed over them, for they keep watch as having to render an account of their souls, so that they may do this with joy and not with grief [see Hebrews 13:7].[1]

—Vatican Council II, *Dogmatic Constitution on the Church*

Prayer

Heavenly Father, thank you for the gift of free will. I know that I can disobey you—you have given me that power—but instead I submit my will to your will. I want to be as Jesus, following your holy directives in all things.

I offer my submission to you as an act of worship, knowing that my obedience is pleasing to you. Accept me as your humble and obedient servant, to the glory of your Holy Name.

Discussion Questions and Action Steps

1. Is there a teaching of the Catholic Church with which you struggle? What is it? How can you learn more about this teaching with the goal of willingly submitting to the authority of the Church instituted by Christ?

2. How well do you submit to rules and regulations in your family, at work, and in society? Do you willingly obey the directives of those in authority?

3. We are encouraged to pray for those in authority over us. For you, who are those persons? Do you pray for them?

"Who's the Boss Here?"

::: On Jesus, Lord of the home :::

My young granddaughter Rebecca was spending the evening with my wife, Libbie, my youngest daughter, Beverly, and me while her parents went out to dinner. We had just finished grace before our meal when Rebecca asked, "Who's the boss of me tonight?"

Smiling I answered, "Your Aunt Bev is in charge of you tonight."

Rebecca, with great seriousness, announced to us, "My daddy is the boss at my house!"

Libbie, Beverly, and I all smiled with that condescending look that adults have when a child says something cute. However, her next question left us all speechless. Rebecca asked, "And who's the boss here?"

Who, indeed, is in charge? I've seen families in which either the mother or father controls the home. More often than I'd like to admit, I've seen homes where some child or the children in general run the house. They can be quite the dictators! Their needs and wants are the determining factors for all activities. I've even seen homes where the family pet seems to rule the roost.

However, for the Catholic family there can be only one "boss." That person is not the husband, not the wife, not the children, and certainly not the family pet. Jesus is the only one with enough love and wisdom to reign in our homes.

The family is the basic cell of society. It's a small kingdom, and any kingdom can have only one king. We need to make sure that Jesus is the one seated on the throne in our homes. That starts by making sure that he is enthroned in our hearts, for he is the benevolent King who only rules when invited.

We can renew our submission to the King each and every morning with the Morning Offering: "Lord, I offer you today everything I think, do, and say." Consciously we place our wills in conformity to his. Next we entrust our families to him, with the intent of seeking his government and obeying his directives.

Since our King is hidden from our physical eyes, it's advantageous to use some tangible sign to remind us of his rule. Putting a crucifix where it will be regularly seen and, perhaps, making a practice of prayerfully bowing whenever passing it is a good approach. Some families keep an empty chair at the head of the table during meals as a reminder of the unseen Guest who daily joins them.

While I was growing up, the most powerful image for me was a picture of the Sacred Heart of Jesus, which hung in a prominent place in our family's living room and was one of the first things I saw upon entering the house. Even as a young child, I knew that his heart bled because of his love for me. It was his love displayed on the cross that I could see in the enflamed heart in that picture. It was obvious too that his love required a response from me.

My parents had "enthroned" Christ in their home. The most important personality in that family of nine was the Lord Jesus.

The Enthronement of the Sacred Heart of Jesus in the Home is a great way to consciously put Christ at the center of the family. It is a simple ceremony in which the entire family can participate. It can be annually renewed with a pageant appropriate for the King of Kings.[1] The ceremony and the picture of the Sacred Heart in a prominent place will be regular reminders to you and your family of who is the boss!

Points to Ponder

You shall not have other gods besides me.

—Exodus 20:3, *NAB*

As I live, says the Lord, every knee shall bend before me,
and every tongue shall give praise to God.

—Romans 14:11, *NAB*

The kingship and empire of Christ have been recognized in the pious custom, practiced by many families, of dedicating themselves to the Sacred Heart of Jesus.[2]

—Pope Pius XI, *Quas Primas*

Prayer

Almighty and eternal Father, we, the [insert family name] family, consecrate ourselves and our home to the Sacred Heart of your only begotten Son, Jesus Christ, Our Lord, who loves us with a tender and everlasting love. May we return this love as he comes into the midst of our family to live and share our life in a special way from this day on.

We freely choose to make this covenant of love with you, Father, and dedicate to the Heart of Jesus all that we have, without any reservation on our part, promising to amend our lives by turning from sin and all that might lead us into sin.

Jesus, we accept you as a living member of our family. Sanctify our joys and comfort us in our sorrows. May your Spirit continually make us aware of your special presence among us and in one another.

Stay with us, Lord, and through this consecration help us to have a deep and loving respect for one another. Help us to imitate your gentle and humble heart, that we may give ourselves to each other by the faithful performance of our family obligations.[3]

Discussion Questions and Action Steps

1. What can you do to help you recall and renew your Morning Offering throughout the day?

2. What in your personal or family life is not under the lordship of Jesus? (Some sin pattern? Television, Internet, or other entertainment? Use of time? Ways of relating?) What can you do to make Jesus Lord in these areas?

3. Part of the commission we have received through our baptism and confirmation is to extend the kingdom of Christ within our sphere of influence. What can you do to extend God's kingdom in your work and social settings?

Flecte Genu
::: On adoring the Lord :::

When I was about seventeen, I injured my right knee while playing basketball. For a variety of reasons, I didn't have the surgery that would have repaired it. More of an inconvenience than a serious problem, I would just wear a brace for physical activity. However, advancing age and a touch of arthritis have increased the problem. Now my knee aches in damp weather and gives out at inconvenient times.

One activity that regularly challenges me is genuflection. I need to hold on to a pew or chair while I slowly lower my right knee until it touches the floor near my left heel—the proper form that my parents and the good sisters at Catholic grade school taught me. I then must struggle, relying on arm strength, to get back to a standing position.

I am thankful for that regular struggle. Genuflection, bending the knee (*flecte genu* in Latin), had for too long been merely a perfunctory action for me. Bob down, make the Sign of the Cross, bob up, and get into the pew. However, genuflection is not meant to be a meaningless ritual. On the contrary, it is an opportunity to make an important statement of faith.

The bending of the knee in genuflection is to be a reflection of a bending of the will. Genuflection is the action of a servant in the presence of his master. It is an act of reverence, worship, and adoration.

In church we genuflect not to a statue, not to the crucifix, and not to the altar. All these are items for due reverence, yet they are mere symbols of greater realities. No, we genuflect to a Person—Jesus, who is truly present, Body, Blood, soul, and divinity, in the tabernacle.

Genuflection positions us appropriately. We have been called by the Lord to come to Mass. We set aside our agendas and look to our King. We will listen to his Word and receive his gift of self in the Eucharist.

Despite knowing that Jesus is present, I still struggle with my thoughts and my flesh, which all too often distract me from what is most important—turning my full attention to the One who has saved me, cares for me now, and has prepared a place for me in his heavenly kingdom. That is why I appreciate my bad knee. I remember that after Jacob struggled with God, he walked with a limp (see Genesis 32:24–31). That limp was a reminder to Jacob of his relationship with the living God.

So blessed be my knee that I cannot ignore! My struggle to fall and rise in genuflection is just what I need. It forces me to focus.

As it is not easy to bend my knee, it surely is not easy to bend my heart and my mind. But I can take up the struggle. I can make an act of the will. "Jesus, I bow before you!"

May I suggest that, the next time your knee touches the floor at your parish church, do not hurry to rise. Turn your focus to him, who in humility that is truly divine is present in the tabernacle. Linger in that position of adoration and submission, and tell your Lord, "I adore you; I worship you; I acknowledge you as King of Kings. And as I bend my knee, so I bend my will. Lord, may your will be done in my life!"

Points to Ponder

The LORD reigns; let the peoples tremble!
>He sits enthroned upon the cherubim; let the earth quake!
The LORD is great in Zion;
>he is exalted over all the peoples.
Let them praise your great and awesome name!
>Holy is he!
Mighty King, lover of justice,
>you have established equity;
you have executed justice
>and righteousness in Jacob.
Extol the LORD our God;
>worship at his footstool!
>Holy is he!

—Psalm 99:1–5

Even bodily adoration is done in spirit, in so far as it proceeds from and is directed to spiritual devotion.

Just as prayer is primarily in the mind, and secondarily expressed in words, ... so too adoration consists chiefly in an interior reverence of God, but secondarily in certain bodily signs of humility; thus when we genuflect we signify our weakness in comparison with God, and when we prostrate ourselves we profess that we are nothing of ourselves.

Though we cannot reach God with the senses, our mind is urged by sensible signs to approach God. [1]

—St. Thomas Aquinas, *Summa Theologica*

Prayer

Decide on a short prayer that you will say when you genuflect to Jesus in the tabernacle at church. Realize that joining the prayer with the action of genuflection brings both your mind and your body into a position of worship. This is the prayer that I regularly use: "I worship you, Jesus, my Lord, my God, my hope, my salvation, my joy, and my all!"

Discussion Questions and Action Steps

1. Genuflection is only one position we use in the presence of God. We stand to hear His Word proclaimed in the Gospel. We kneel at the Consecration. How can you better use those postures for prayer?

2. In the Mass we are given many opportunities to focus on God. What are some of those opportunities, and how can you better take advantage of them?

3. How can you incorporate prayers of adoration, praise, and worship into your prayer life?

An Answer in the Mail
::: On discernment :::

The stress of my job was affecting my health. The long hours were also taking me away from Libbie and our four children. It was in this environment that my wife and I came to the realization that something had to change. I needed to either make adjustments at my present job or find other employment. So we began to ask God what he would want us to do.

I regularly surveyed the local want ads, always with a prayer to the Holy Spirit for wisdom. A notice in a professional magazine caught my eye. However, the job was in Tucson, far from our roots in western Pennsylvania. That alone gave us pause. Our children would need to leave good Catholic schools and friends. We would be the first in our extended family to move from the area, leaving that loving and supportive environment. We hadn't seriously considered such a move.

Yet after Libbie and I discussed the possibility, we decided to prayerfully make inquiries. I called an acquaintance who worked for the diocese that was looking for the new hire. He told me that he would be involved in deciding whom to hire and would be that person's immediate supervisor. He was enthusiastic about the prospect of my having the job. So I applied, asking God to close doors if this was not the right move for our family.

The initial two interviews were positive, and likewise a visit to Tucson. During this time Libbie and I talked with our children and extended family about the possible move. Though they expressed a certain normal anxiety, everyone was open to the possibility. I also spoke regularly with my spiritual director. His support, encouragement, advice, and prayers were of great help. Libbie and I continued our prayers, including a novena.[1]

Then came the offer. It was time for a decision. Would we take the offer and move to Tucson? Was this really what God wanted us to do?

We again gathered as a family to review our time of discernment. Certainly God had opened doors. Our prayers and the advice of others had been pointing us in the direction of accepting the offer. Yet we wanted to be sure. We offered one more prayer: "Lord, we want to do your will. It seems to us that you are directing us to take this job in Tucson. However, it is such an important and life-changing decision; we ask that you give us a sign that this truly is your will for us."

The next day I found a letter in the mailbox from a priest who had taught me in high school. I had maintained casual communication with him over the years. However, it had been a long time since I had heard from him, so it was somewhat of a surprise to receive that letter. On closer inspection I saw that the letter was postmarked Tucson. Father was writing to tell me that he had been transferred to Arizona.

My wife and I could only bow our heads and thank God for his gracious mercy. He had honored our request and given us this last sign, so that we would know that, indeed, we were walking in his will.

The arrival of that letter did not determine the verdict for us. No, we arrived at the decision after a time of discernment. But that letter was a confirmation that helped us take the last step in a whole-hearted yes to God.

How to Discern God's Direction for Your Life

Discernment—hearing God's direction for a specific decision—is not a science. You can't do A, then observe B, and come to conclusion C. God is not a calculator or machine. God is a Trinity of three Persons to whom we relate.

Building a relationship is an art, not a science. We would not want it otherwise. We don't want our relationship with our spouse or best friend to be a science project; we want our close relationships to be founded on love, with the communication, interplay, time-tested commitment, and ongoing connection that love entails. It is no less with God. That is why hearing God is often so difficult. It is also why it is so wonderful.

God knows each of us intimately. He deals with us as individuals. As we respond to him, we draw closer to him; we grow to know and love him better. We are on a journey to the eternal embrace of divine love that awaits us on the other side of the grave.

Yet even though discernment is not a science, that does not mean we can't identify key components of the process.

- First, if we want to hear from God, we need commitment to his will—the pledge to obey him when he speaks. God does not expect purity of intention. He knows we are sinners who still struggle with fears. But he does want us to have the desire to obey, like the man in the Gospel who prayed, "I believe, help my unbelief" (Mark 9:24).

- God has already revealed his will for many parts of our lives. For example, there is no need to ask God if I should attend Mass on Sunday or, if I'm validly married, whether I should stay married.[2]

- Seek God's direction where he has already spoken to his people: Scripture, Church teaching, and the sacraments, especially reconciliation and the Eucharist.

- Ask for God's direction, and listen. Here ongoing, faithful prayer is important, since it builds our relationship with God.

- Seek godly counsel. A spiritual director or a trusted, mature Catholic advisor is often invaluable in sorting through alternatives.

- Cultivate the witness of a well-formed conscience.

- Look for interior signs (movements of the Spirit, a sense of peace, clarity replacing confusion).

- Look for external signs (doors opening, the agreement of others close to you).

No one of the above is sufficient in and of itself, but in combination they will help you discern God's will. Again, discernment is not a science project but the fruit of a vital, ongoing relationship with God.

One good book that further covers this process is *Discerning the Will of God: An Ignatian Guide to Christian Decision Making* by Timothy M. Gallagher (Crossroad, 2009).

Points to Ponder

> The LORD is near to all who call upon him,
> to all who call upon him in truth.
>
> —Psalm 145:18

"Come to him [Christ], a living stone" (1 Peter 2:4). Yes, dear brothers and sisters, make sure that Christ the Lord is your teacher and also your children's. It is from him that you should draw the right criteria for direction and discernment in every situation. [3]

—Blessed Pope John Paul II, Homily
"True Human Love Reflects the Divine"

Prayer

Our Father, who art in heaven,
Hallowed be thy name.
Thy kingdom come.
thy will be done, on earth as it is in heaven.
Give us this day our daily bread.
And forgive us our trespasses,
as we forgive those who trespass against us.
And lead us not into temptation,
but deliver us from evil. Amen. (emphasis added)

Discussion Questions and Action Steps

1. What examples can you recall from the lives of scriptural personages or of the saints that show how God guided people?
2. Recall your own testimony. How has God guided you in the past?
3. What decisions do you face now? How can you seek to know and obey God's will?

A Delayed Response

::: On the sacrament of confirmation :::

Baptism and confirmation are closely linked sacraments. The latter is a completion of the former. By the sacrament of baptism the recipient becomes an adopted son or daughter of God. Sin is forgiven, and grace is bestowed to enable the baptized to live and act according to the plan and will of God. "Confirmation brings an increase and deepening of baptismal grace" (*CCC*, #1303). By the grace of this sacrament, the confirmed is empowered not only to live the faith but also to spread and defend it.

In the Eastern rites of the Catholic Church, the two sacraments are administered at the same time. In the Roman rite they are administered at the same time for adult converts, usually at the Easter Vigil Mass, but for those who are baptized as infants, confirmation is only administered after the person has reached the age of reason.[1]

I was confirmed in eighth grade. I don't remember much about the day. I can't recall feeling any particular emotion, sensation, or enlightenment. I do have an old photo showing me dressed in a black suit.

I knew all the names of the gifts and the fruits of the Holy Spirit—we had learned them and their meanings during our time of preparation for the sacrament. I didn't take any giant steps in living them after the bishop had anointed my forehead, laid hands on my head, and given me a gentle slap on the cheek. Intellectually I knew I was being called to a more dedicated witness to the faith. I was to be a soldier of Christ, ready for martyrdom if that were ever required of me.

Even though I didn't see big changes in my life at the confirmation service or in the time immediately after, I can say without hesitation that my reception of this sacrament was a life-changing event. When I rose from my kneeling position before the bishop and walked back to my pew, I was a changed man. I had been given an increase of grace. My soul was marked indelibly with what the *Catechism* refers to as a "character" (see *CCC*, #1304).

How can I say this after I just told you of how little I felt the change? It is because I know that the sacraments, when administered according to the Church's directives, which Christ gave to the first apostles, are always effective. The seven sacraments give grace. You can put extra emphasis on the period in that declarative sentence. There are no "ifs" involved. Christ always is a man of his word. He gives grace through the sacraments, regardless of whether the recipient feels anything or not.

Of course, that begs a question. If grace was given, why didn't I experience it in perceptible ways? The answer? God gave the grace, but I was not receptive enough to experience its life-changing power at that time in my life. It took me some time to catch up with the work that God had done in and for me at my confirmation.

Embracing the Grace

Flash forward about four years. I was a senior in high school. As is common with high school students, I was confused. From my earliest years, inspired by many good priests in my parish and by two uncles who were priests, I had wanted to be a priest. I was, in fact, attending a pre-seminary high school. Yet the young ladies had also caught my eye. There was one young woman who particularly held my attention.

There was also the specter of the draft and Vietnam that hung over all high school males at that time. And while I never doubted the love of my parents, my relationship with them, especially with my dad, was strained. This was the baggage that I carried with me when I went on a weekend retreat with my classmates.

I didn't know what to expect. It was my first weekend retreat, and I was instructed to maintain silence during it. The retreat director explained that the silence was maintained so that we could hear God. I wasn't at all sure what that meant. All I knew was that I needed God or someone—anyone—to help me find my way through the maze that I was in.

After one session the retreat director gave us an assignment. We were to read some passages from the Gospel of John in the privacy of our rooms. We were also to ask God to speak to us! Again, I wasn't at all sure how I was supposed to "hear" God, but I was willing to give it a try.

So I read the Scriptures, closed my Bible, and asked God to speak to me. He did.

I didn't hear an audible voice from a corner of the room. There were no visions. Yet as sure as I know that my fingers are touching the keypad as I type these words, I know God spoke to me that day. How? It's not easy to describe, but here is my best shot.

Physically it felt as if someone was touching me from the inside out. I knew at that moment that I was a sinner but that God loved me and wanted to lead me closer to him. I knew those facts beyond questioning at that moment.

Finally, I had clarity where before confusion had reigned. It wasn't that I had all of the specific answers to the questions that burdened me. Instead I experienced a peace in knowing that there was a plan and a direction for me and that God would lead me.

For my part I repented for my sins. I told God that I accepted his love and that I wanted to love him with all of my being. I promised that I would do whatever he asked of me. I knew he had given himself totally to me and I was to do the same—give myself to him. Then I wept unabashedly. They were tears of relief and of joy, and they were cried in the embrace of my heavenly Father, with the hand of my elder brother Jesus on my shoulder, and with the Holy Spirit in my heart.[2]

Our evangelical Christian brothers and sisters would say that I had a conversion experience. I'd turned from sin and self and accepted Jesus as my Lord and Savior. There is much truth in that perspective, but it is incomplete. In retrospect I realize that the grace of the sacrament of confirmation had flowered in my life. That grace had been given to me at my parish church on an evening during my eighth year of grade school while I knelt before the shepherd of my diocese. Period. However, it had taken me four more years to catch up with that grace. God had been working in me all of that time and preparing me to finally run to his embrace.

Never Too Late

It is never too late to tap into the graces of the sacraments that are given to us only once. In baptism, confirmation, holy orders, and marriage,[3] God visits us with gifts that keep on giving. Sometimes it takes us time to catch up with what God has already done. Sometimes we wander. Sometimes we sin mortally and need sacramental confession to unbind us. We change; our responses vary; we grow in understanding. We change, but God remains the same. It's a healthy exercise to consider those once-in-a-lifetime sacraments that we have received—to remind ourselves that God does not withdraw what he has given. It is we who fail to respond. However, each moment of each day, we have the opportunity to lay claim to what we have received and allow God to strengthen and guide us through his grace.

Points to Ponder

The fruit of the Spirit is love, joy, peace, patience, kindness, goodness, faithfulness, gentleness, self-control.

—Galatians 5:22–23

The sacraments are efficacious signs of grace, instituted by Christ and entrusted to the Church, by which divine life is dispensed to us. The visible rites by which the sacraments are celebrated signify and make present the graces proper to each sacrament. They bear fruit in those who receive them with the required dispositions.

—*Catechism of the Catholic Church*, #1131

Prayer

Lord, thank you that you are faithful and true. I know that you have blessed me through the sacraments that I have received. You have been patient with me when I have been slow to respond. At this moment—in this prayer—I affirm that you are my Lord and Savior. I desire to yield to you, follow you, and obey you.

Let the favor that you so generously give be the means of my accepting more fully your gracious work in my life. I know that all is grace, and that you always await my yes to it. I declare my yes now to you. Work in my life according to your good will and your pleasure. Amen.

Discussion Questions and Action Steps

1. When were you confirmed? What was your experience at the reception of the sacrament?

2. The gifts of the Holy Spirit are wisdom, understanding, counsel, fortitude, knowledge, piety, and fear of the Lord. Pick one and research its meaning. How well has this gift taken root in your life? Over the next week or month, daily ask the Holy Spirit to build you up in that gift.

3. Reread the fruits of the Holy Spirit listed in this chapter's "Points to Ponder." Which fruit is most established in your life? How can you use that fruit to further God's kingdom?

What I Have I Give to You?

::: On being an instrument of God's mercy :::

I can't point to a particular day when I gave my life to Jesus. As I look at the span of my life, I can see God's merciful hand throughout it. That is not to say, however, that there weren't pivotal moments. Indeed, there are unforgettable incidents that stand out— times that changed, affirmed, or redirected me.

As I mentioned in the previous chapter, one such experience happened while I was on retreat as a senior in high school. On that retreat I powerfully encountered God and decided that my life was his and that I would seek to serve Our Lord and live for him. Consequently I decided to enter the seminary and pursue the priesthood. For me, at that time, service to God translated into the priesthood.

Also on that senior retreat, I was invited to work as a volunteer in Appalachia for part of the summer. I sensed that this opportunity was also part of where God was directing me. My parents graciously gave their approval, and I was on my way.

I and the other volunteers slept on the floor of an old school building at the Catholic parish. My normal daily schedule was as follows: In the morning I'd teach catechism to fourth graders; In the afternoon I would be dropped off at villages with quaint names such as Snuff Hollow and Louise. (There the goal was to give a Catholic witness to the inhabitants, who were usually either Baptist or not affiliated with any denomination); In the evening I'd return to the rectory for dinner and afterward participate in programs and activities for high school students.

I started with great enthusiasm. After all, I had experienced God's love in a powerful way on that senior class retreat, and I wanted to share it with others. My enthusiasm was tempered when confronted with reality.

With the fourth graders it was a struggle just to keep order in the classroom. The poverty of the people I met each afternoon was overwhelming. All I could do was organize activities for the children to give the moms some reprieve. I was only a couple years older than the high school students with whom I worked in the evening. I desperately wanted them to know Jesus and the Church as I did. Unfortunately, they didn't seem very interested in what I had to say about God. Rather their thoughts and energy seemed to center on relationships with the opposite sex, sports, television, and food.

My frustration and self-doubt grew daily. It culminated one afternoon in one of those out-of-the-way Appalachian villages. I was playing with the children when a group of women approached me. One woman was weeping. The spokeswoman for the group said, "You're a minister, aren't you?"

Conscious of my goal to be a Catholic witness, I replied "No, I'm a seminarian studying to be a Catholic priest."

The woman responded, "Well, you're going to be a minister?"

Again, to emphasize my Catholic faith, I replied, "I'm going to be a Catholic priest."

"Well, that's like a minister, isn't it?" she replied.

I conceded at this point. She then pointed to the sobbing woman and told me, "This woman's daughter has just been sent home from Children's Hospital in Pittsburgh, because there is nothing they can do for the child. They say she is going to die."

As I listened I was frantically searching for what words of condolence I could say in response. However, the spokeswoman had more to say. "Since you are going to be a minister, we want you to lay hands on the girl so that she will be healed."

I can't express the terror I felt at those words. This woman actually thought I could heal this girl whom the best hospital in the area said was sure to die. I do not remember what I said next. I only remember that I got out of there as fast as I could. I walked down the dirt road that eventually led to a paved road where I would be picked up later, leaving a sobbing woman with a dying daughter leaning for support on other women.

At dinner that evening I told the story to the parish priest and my fellow volunteers. Seeking to support and comfort me, they said that these folks had a simple faith and took the Bible literally. I shouldn't let that upset me. But those words sounded hollow in my ears. I had come to bring Jesus to these people and had only been able to organize a few games with the children. When they finally brought me a need that they felt a "man of God" could address, I left town with my tail tucked between my legs. They had asked for what only God could give, and my hands and heart were empty.

The day was not yet over. I still had a program for the teens that evening. The pastor had invited a charismatic prayer group to come and hold a prayer meeting in the church.

The prayer group gathered in a circle of chairs in the sanctuary, while the students filled the pews. This was my first exposure to a charismatic prayer meeting, complete with loud praise, prophecy, and praying in tongues. The high school students around me were laughing and making fun of the group. It was culture shock for me. This form of prayer was not like anything I had previously experienced.

Mentally I wanted to write off these charismatics as kooks. Yet I felt spiritual tugs on my heart. The contrast between the sadness at my failures of the day and the joy and exuberance of the members of the prayer group struck me powerfully. Were they merely deluded, or did they have something that I lacked? While I tried to process this dichotomy, a young man, probably only a few years older than I, stood up and gave a testimony of how God had physically healed him.

I was a person who had control of his emotions. In particular I would seldom cry. Yet as I listened, something broke within me. I was not only crying; I was weeping and sobbing, while the teens looked at me in wonderment.

A revelation came to me—perhaps what those charismatics called the spiritual gift of wisdom. I knew in those moments that there was a marked difference between me and those people in the sanctuary. I had been trying to serve God on my terms, with only my natural talents and gifts. In contrast, the men and women in that prayer meeting were yielding to God's work. He was able to work in and through them with a power that was far beyond the natural.

At that moment, in that church, with the tears streaming down my face, I asked God to help me serve not merely with my own strength but rather with his grace and power. In the business world they may say that I experienced a "paradigm shift." More than thirty-five years later, I'm still working out the ramifications of that change in thinking and its implications for how I live my life.

Infused With the Supernatural

There is a Scripture in Mark that I found puzzling until a priest gave me some insight:

> [Jesus] was hungry. And seeing in the distance a fig tree in leaf, he went to see if he could find anything on it. When he came to it, he found nothing but leaves, for it was not the season for figs. And he said to it, "May no one ever eat fruit from you again." And his disciples heard it....
>
> As they passed by in the morning, they saw the fig tree withered away to its roots. And Peter remembered and said to him, "Master, look! The fig tree which you cursed has withered." And Jesus answered them, "Have faith in God. Truly, I say to you, whoever says to this mountain, 'Be taken up and cast into the sea,' and does not doubt in his heart, but believes that what he says will come to pass, it will be done for him." (Mark 11:12–14; 20–23)

That fig tree was doing what was normal for it. In the natural order of things, it was not the time for fruit. But Jesus was looking for something more. He was looking for spiritual fruit.

That is the lesson he pointed out to the disciples. In the merely natural realm, their power was limited. However, as men of faith, they could approach God and find a whole new level of reality. God had supernatural power for them that could move mountains. As Jesus would tell his disciples on another occasion, "With men this is impossible, but with God all things are possible" (Matthew 19:26).

Points to Ponder

Now Peter and John were going up to the temple at the hour of prayer, the ninth hour. And a man lame from birth was being carried, whom they laid daily at that gate of the temple which is called Beautiful to ask alms of those who entered the temple. Seeing Peter and John about to go into the temple, he asked for alms. And Peter directed his gaze at him, with John, and said, "Look at us." And he fixed his attention upon them, expecting to receive something from them. But Peter said, "I have no silver and gold, but I give you what I have; in the name of Jesus Christ of Nazareth, walk." And he took him by the right hand and raised him up; and immediately his feet and ankles were made strong. And leaping up he stood and walked and entered the temple with them, walking and leaping and praising God. And all the people saw him walking and praising God.

—Acts 3:1–9

All that Jesus had begun to do with his followers in the three years of their life together is brought to fulfillment by the gift of the Spirit. The apostles' faith is at first imperfect and hesitant, but later becomes strong and fruitful: he causes the lame to walk (see Acts 3:1–10), while he puts to flight unclean spirits (Acts 5:16).... They who had learned from Jesus so imperfectly and with such difficulty how to pray, love and go out on mission, now truly pray, truly love, are truly missionaries and truly apostles.

This is the work that the Spirit of Jesus accomplishes in his Apostles![1]

—Blessed Pope John Paul II, Message on the Occasion of the 13th World Youth Day

Prayer

Lord, I know that you desire to work miracles for people so that they will know the joy and love that come from a relationship with you. I know also that it is your will to accomplish your work through those who yield themselves to you. Knowing that my "strength" is really only weakness, I desire to be a conduit of your grace and a tool in your hands, and to serve by your strength. May all that I am and all that I do be in accordance with your will and for your glory. Amen.

Discussion Questions and Action Steps

1. Where do you need the manifestation of God's power in your life? Have you been trying to "do it on your own"? Ask someone to pray with you and for you.

2. Recall how God has worked through you to bless someone in the past. Give a prayerful witness by telling someone about the incident.

3. Peter and John gave what they had to the blind man at the temple entrance. What do you have to give to others? Is it some material item, a word of encouragement, time, prayer, or something else? Plan to share from your bounty.

A Healthy Shot in the Arm

::: On accountability and confession :::

I enjoy playing basketball. I started while in grade school, and I still shoot a few hoops even today. However, I did pick up a bad habit while playing basketball in college. When I missed a shot, committed a foul, or failed to grab a rebound, I often added a verbal vulgarity to the situation. In this respect I fit in with the rest of the team; most of the guys used "colorful" language.

I did feel a certain justification in that I never cursed or blasphemed. No, my offenses were the garden-variety vulgarities.[1] Nonetheless, when another Catholic friend on the team suggested we clean up our language, I was duly convicted of my failings and agreed.

We both knew that we needed some incentive to triumph over what had become an automatic response. So we agreed that each time we uttered an offensive word or phrase, we would throw a quarter in a bucket. We would save the money and send it to a charity.

We did make progress, but in a very short time, we realized that this approach was too expensive! A quarter meant something to a poor college student back then.

My friend had another suggestion. Rather than a financial penalty, he suggested a corporal one. During practice or a game, we would keep track of our offenses, and afterwards we would administer one solid punch to the other's shoulder for each foul utterance. There was one problem. I was a five-foot-seven guard who weighed about 120 pounds. He was a much taller, solidly built forward who weighed roughly fifty pounds more than me.

When I administered my best punch to his arm, he seemed to barely feel it. In fact, on occasion he exhorted me to greater effort. Meanwhile, his punches just about knocked me over. Both of my shoulders were quickly turning black and blue. Consequently, in just a few days I was cured! The most I might utter on a missed play was a muffled groan. To this day the use of vulgarities does not plague me.

I learned two important lessons. First, it's not wise to allow someone significantly bigger to punch you with impunity. More importantly, I learned about brotherhood and its effectiveness in overcoming sinful tendencies.

Accountability

Being a "lone ranger" Christian is not a good idea. The "only me and Jesus" approach to faith is actually downright dangerous to a person's spiritual health. Jesus established a Church, and membership in that Church is a very important component of Christian life. As members of the body of Christ, grace flows to us not only directly from God but also through our brothers and sisters. As Scripture tells us, there are a variety of gifts, and when we work in concert with others, we all benefit from the sharing of those gifts (see 1 Corinthians 12). In the body we receive encouragement, support, correction, perspective, and much more.

In the body you and I are called to be accountable. First of all, I am culpable before God. When I sin I offend him. When the sin is serious, I break communion with God; with less serious sin I wound my relationship with him.

Additionally, what I do, whether good or evil, affects the rest of the body. As Paul writes, "God has so composed the body...that the members may have the same care for one another. If one member suffers, all suffer together; if one member is honored, all rejoice together" (1 Corinthians 12:24–26).

So I must accept blame that is rightfully mine. That is one of many reasons why the sacrament of reconciliation is so valuable. I confess my sins to a priest. By the grace that he has received through the sacrament of holy orders, he stands in the place of Christ. I hear Christ's words of forgiveness through the vocal cords of an ordained man.

That priest, through whom Christ works the ministry of mercy, also represents the entire people of God. I can't e-mail every believer, apologizing for my failings and asking forgiveness; but I can accomplish that *mea culpa* (Latin for "through my fault") when I confess to one who not only stands in place of Christ but also represents every man.

My repentance in confession must be sincere; that is one of the requirements of the sacrament. I must want to change for the better. Yet we know that our human nature is weak. We often fall again. So we return to confession, again seek God's forgiveness, and apologize to God's family.

The sacrament of reconciliation is an exercise in accountability. It is similar to admitting to my basketball friend that I failed. Like that punch to the shoulder, confession is not a fun experience, but it is a vital means of overcoming my sins, failings, and faults. In fact, it is absolutely necessary when my sins are of the mortal type. Like that punch, those times of confession can move me forward to my goal of becoming a better, godlier man.

There is, however, a difference between the accountability of a shot to the arm and the shot to the soul through confession. The former left me black and blue. The latter gives me grace that leaves me cleansed, renewed, and strengthened.

Points to Ponder

If we confess our sins, he is faithful and just, and will forgive our sins and cleanse us from all unrighteousness.

—1 John 1:9

One who desires to obtain reconciliation with God and with the Church must confess to a priest all the unconfessed grave sins he remembers.... The confession of venial faults, without being necessary in itself, is nevertheless strongly recommended by the Church.

—*Catechism of the Catholic Church*, #1493

Prayer

The Act of Contrition

O my God, I am heartily sorry for having offended Thee,
and I detest all my sins,
because I dread the loss of heaven, and the pains of hell;
but most of all because they offend Thee, my God,
Who are all good and deserving of all my love.
I firmly resolve, with the help of Thy grace,
to confess my sins, to do penance, and to amend my life. Amen.

Discussion Questions and Action Steps

1. Is there a pattern of sin in your life that you have made progress in overcoming? What has helped you make that progress?

2. Review what the *Catechism* says about the sacrament of reconciliation (see *CCC*, #1422–1470). When is confession necessary? What are the necessary components of the sacrament?

3. What are the spiritual effects of the sacrament of reconciliation (see *CCC*, #1496)?

Isn't That Nice?

::: On pleasing God, not men :::

"OK, boys, I'm giving you a list of the names of your fellow students. Next to each name I want you to write your impression of that individual."

It was a project for our senior religion class at my all-male high school. After we finished the project, the religion teacher, a Jesuit priest, met individually with each of us to review the comments. When my turn arrived, I sat in his office with considerable apprehension. What did my fellow classmates write about me?

Father organized his papers and began: "Regis, the comments concerning you were the most consistent in the class. Almost everyone said that they didn't know you well but that they viewed you as a 'nice guy.'"

I started to give a sigh of relief, but Father continued: "Tell me, Rege, what is a nice guy? Isn't that just someone who doesn't make a difference?"

He was right. I always avoided making waves. I tried to please everyone. Being nice was definitely my goal. And as I considered the matter, I was convinced that he was also right in his last statement. I didn't make a difference in anyone's life.

We all have a desire to be liked. However, as witnesses for Christ, we are not measured by whether we are nice. Our standards are truth, faithfulness, and the same love that motivated Jesus. Elisabeth Elliot, evangelist and author, says that as Christians we need an A.U.G. degree—"Approved unto God."[1]

We strive not to satisfy other men and women but to please God. This means that at times we need to speak strong words—words that may cause us to be unpopular—and take actions that won't be appreciated. Jesus had strong words for the Pharisees, whom he called "blind guides" and "hypocrites" (see Matthew 23:13–33). He overturned the tables of the money-changers because they had made God's house a den of thieves (Matthew 21:12–13; Mark 11:15–18; Luke 19:45–46; John 2:13–17). I'm sure the Pharisees and money-changers didn't consider Jesus a "nice guy" after these events.

Jesus perhaps reached the pinnacle of popularity during his earthly ministry when he miraculously fed the multitude with bread and fish (see John 6:1–14). Free food is always appreciated! Not long afterwards Jesus gave one of his most unpopular teachings: "I say to you, unless you eat the flesh of the Son of man and drink his blood, you have no life in you" (John 6:53). The effect of his words? "Many of his disciples, when they heard it, said, 'This is a hard saying; who can listen to it?'" (John 6:60). In fact, "many of his disciples drew back and no longer went about with him" (John 6:66). So much for popularity!

Sometimes our words may be softly spoken but unpopular nonetheless. Rather than join in stoning the woman caught in adultery, Jesus bent down and wrote on the ground. While the crowd planned to manifest anger and hatred, Jesus offered forgiveness and peace (see John 8:3–11).

Being motivated by other's opinions of us will inhibit our ability to witness in word and deed. St. Paul encourages us: "Do not conform yourself to this age but be transformed by the renewal of your mind, that you may discern what is the will of God" (Romans 12:2, *NAB*). When we have the mind of Christ and are motivated by his Spirit, we may suffer rejection. St. Peter reminds us: "But even if you do suffer for righteousness' sake, you will be blessed. Have no fear of them, nor be troubled, but in your hearts reverence Christ as Lord. Always be prepared to make a defense to any one who calls you to account for the hope that is in you, yet do it with gentleness and reverence; and keep your conscience clear, so that, when you are abused, those who revile your good behavior in Christ may be put to shame" (1 Peter 3:14–16).

I think I am still a "nice guy," but I am different from the pleasant young man that I was in high school. Now my goal is not to be nice but to follow God's will and love him in all I say and do.

Points to Ponder

Am I now seeking the favor of men, or of God? Or am I trying to please men? If I were still pleasing men, I should not be a servant of Christ.

—Galatians 1:10

We speak, not to please men, but to please God who tests our hearts.

—1 Thessalonians 2:4

[W]hat end did St. Paul have in his preaching? Not to please men, but Christ.... As his heart was on fire with the love of Christ, he sought for nothing save the glory of Christ. O that all...engaged in the ministry of the Word were true lovers of Jesus Christ. [2]

—Pope Benedict XV, *Encyclical Letter on Preaching the Word of God*

Prayer

I must admit, Lord, that I desire the approval of men. Rejection hurts. Yet, Jesus, I desire your approval more. I desire to please you in all that I do and say. Fortify me, that I may have the courage to stand—even if it means standing alone—in order to live and proclaim the truth.

Guide me by your Holy Spirit, that my life would give you glory. And heavenly Father, please grant me consolation when I most need it, so that I not falter but persevere.

Discussion Questions and Action Steps

1. Have you compromised the truth so that others would not think ill of you? What were the circumstances? How did you feel? What was the outcome?
2. What are the issues today about which Catholics must take an unpopular stance?
3. Being "nice" is not a virtue, but integrity, justice, charity, and courage are virtues. How can you foster them in your life?

"Who Are You Talkin' To?"
::: On addressing God in prayer :::

Family prayer has been an important part of the routine in our home. How we pray has changed over the years, based on the stages of development of our children. When our three oldest children were small, we would say a few rote prayers in the evening, and then I would ask them a couple questions, including, "Bridget (or Clare or Regis), for what do you want to thank God today?"

The child would then respond, "Jesus, thank you for the beautiful weather today," or for whatever was important to the child during that particular day. I always required them to address God (that is, "Jesus" or "Father" or "Lord," or simply "God"). If they neglected the direct address, I would ask, "To whom are you speaking?" The child (usually my son, the youngest of the three) would then restate the prayer of thanks with the appropriate manner of address.

On one occasion one of my wife's sisters was visiting us. She was not a practicing Catholic; actually she was an agnostic. She lived out of town, so she did not visit often. When it came time for night prayers, I explained our routine and invited her to join us. She said she would be delighted.

When it came to the point of giving thanks, I asked if she would like to give thanks for something from the day. She answered, "I'm thankful for this wonderful family." The pause was fairly brief before our five-year-old son yelled, "And who are you talkin' to?"

What is that saying about "out of the mouths of babes"? The situation was a bit uncomfortable, but my young son had spoken an important truth. When we pray we do not fling meaningless words into the air. No, we turn and face God. We raise our hearts and our minds to him, and to him we bend our wills. We address neither the wall nor some picture nor the sky. We address a Person.

When we address Jesus, we speak to the Second Person of the Holy Trinity—he who took on flesh, becoming man to save us from our personal sins and from the sin that we inherited as a consequence of the original sin of our first ancestors. We also acknowledge that he is our brother because through baptism we entered into his death and resurrection and into the family of God.

When we speak to Jesus as Lord, we submit our lives to him, acknowledging our place as the redeemed before the Redeemer. We recognize our debt to him who broke the bonds that enslaved us. At the same time we place ourselves before him as servants, knowing also that he calls us his friends.

Indeed, when we begin to pray, it is most appropriate to pause and recall to whom we speak. Rather than plunge headlong into intercession, contrition, thanksgiving, or even praise, we lift our spiritual gaze to look at God. Only then do we begin to speak.

In addition to speaking to Jesus, we can address our heavenly Father. His arms are open to us. In his will we find the meaning, purpose, and goal of our lives.

We can also address the Holy Spirit. He is the Paraclete—advocate, intercessor, teacher, helper, and comforter. Sent by the ascended Christ and the Father, the Third Person of the Trinity is very near to us. In fact, when we are in the state of grace, he even resides within us.

We are blessed to have a personal relationship with God and are invited to call upon him as such. As the psalmist wrote, "Because [the Lord] inclined his ear to me, therefore I will call on him as long as I live" (Psalm 116:2).

Points to Ponder
> Pray then like this:
> *Our Father*, who art in heaven,
> Hallowed be thy name.
> > —Matthew 6:9, emphasis added

> Hear my prayer, O LORD; give ear to my supplications!
> > —Psalm 143:1, emphasis added

> The twenty-four elders fall down before him who is seated on the throne and worship him who lives for ever and ever; they cast their crowns before the throne, singing,
> "Worthy are you, *our Lord and God*,
> to receive glory and honor and power,
> for you created all things,
> and by your will they existed and were created."
> > —Revelation 4:10–11, emphasis added

> In the New Covenant, prayer is the living relationship of the children of God with their Father who is good beyond measure, with his Son Jesus Christ and with the Holy Spirit.
> > —*Catechism of the Catholic Church*, #2565

Prayer

My Lord and my God, thank you for my personal relationship with you. Thank you that you know me fully and love me intimately. Let me never take you for granted. Instead, sharpen my focus so that I can see you better. Help me to daily know the joy of relating to you— my Father; my brother, Jesus; and the Holy Spirit who lives within me. May my relationship with you deepen during this life so that I am fully ready to meet you face to face in heaven.

Discussion Questions and Action Steps

1. Do you set aside time each day for prayer? Are the place and time of prayer assists or hindrances to prayer? What changes could you make in order to be more faithful and more present to God in prayer?

2. How do you address God in prayer? Take some time to reflect on each Person of the Trinity. List some attributes of each Person.

3. Jesus told his disciples, "I no longer call you slaves, because a slave does not know what his master is doing. I have called you friends" (John 15:15). List some of the work that the Master is doing in your life. What will you ask your friend Jesus to do to help you in this work?

Poverty, Thanksgiving, Generosity, and Joy
::: On poverty of spirit :::

For a couple years I worked as a "paid beggar" for Catholic Charities. One of my duties was to speak to groups of employees at various businesses each autumn, encouraging them to give to United Way through payroll deductions and asking them to designate Catholic Charities as the recipient of their gifts.

The reactions to my pleas were fairly predictable. If attendance at my presentation was voluntary, I often spoke to very small numbers; sometimes no one showed. If it was mandatory for employees to attend, there were always people in the audience who ignored me, spoke to those around them throughout my talk, or on occasion showed outward hostility. More than once I was told, "If the company wants me to donate my money, they should pay me more."

Don't get me wrong here. I also encountered generous and kind people, but unfortunately they were usually in the minority.

There was one large business where I spoke to many groups of employees—electricians, office clerks, warehouse staff, and so on.

They worked three shifts, so I visited at all hours of the day and night. As I was drawing to the end of the list of scheduled talks, I asked the United Way coordinator at the company if there were any other groups to whom I could speak. She told me, "Well, there are the custodians. There are only twelve, and they are the lowest paid employees, so you probably don't want to make a special trip to speak with them."

I hesitated, but since my *modus operandi* was to speak to anyone who would listen, I told the coordinator that I would be happy to return the next day to address the custodians. It was an auspicious decision.

The following day, when I walked into the meeting room, my first thought was that I had made a mistake. The twelve individuals in the room looked more like people who needed the services of Catholic Charities rather than people who could donate to the work. Everyone in the room had some form of mental or physical challenge. One man was missing an arm. One woman was deaf. Another had a shriveled arm. An older gentleman with legs of differing lengths could only walk by forcefully throwing his body to make his shorter leg move forward.

I found myself talking with this older gentleman. He told me how happy he was to work for the company. In all his many years of employment, he had only missed one scheduled day of work, and that was due to a blizzard that had paralyzed the city. He was thankful for those who had given him rides over the years—he couldn't drive—and for the bus service. Throughout our brief conversation he wore a steady smile and exuded joy.

This man would be retiring in January—only a few months away. Because he never took a sick day and seldom took a vacation day, he had accumulated a considerable amount of unpaid time. In fact, he told me that he would receive his regular pay for three months after he retired—the maximum that an employee could accumulate. It was obvious to me that those three months were only a small portion of the time that he had actually accumulated.

We stopped talking when the coordinator asked everyone to sit, and she introduced me. I again knew that this was not the usual crowd when everyone who was physically able to do so applauded! It isn't often that people are happy to see someone who wants to get into their purses or wallets.

You could have heard a pin drop as I spoke. They were the most attentive audience I had ever encountered. The deaf woman had made a point of sitting where she could best read my lips.

I finished my talk as I always did, by passing out the donation forms and telling my audience that I would be happy to help anyone who needed assistance in completing the forms. As I stepped away from the podium, there was again sincere applause.

Then something truly amazing happened. Everyone started to complete the forms or seek my help because their physical infirmity made it difficult or impossible to write. My elderly friend was waiting patiently to speak with me. He had one question that was important to him: How could he make sure that the deduction was taken from his pay during the three months after he retired? My awe at the generosity of this man, combined with that of his fellow custodians, reached its fullness, and my tears began to flow.

They flow now as I type this story for you. Every custodian in that room had signed up to contribute. They were the lowest paid and the most apparently in need. In a word, they were poor. Nevertheless, they were the most thankful, generous, and joyful.

That presentation, which I almost bypassed, changed me and taught me. I already knew that we are called to be thankful in all situations. It's a scriptural injunction: "Rejoice always, pray constantly, give thanks in all circumstances; for this is the will of God in Christ Jesus for you" (1 Thessalonians 5:16–18). However, I would have been inclined to connect prosperity with thankfulness and joy. Experience and the Scriptures have taught me otherwise.

It is often those who lack material wealth, physical health, or the benefits of good employment, social status, or what we would call "the good life" who are the most thankful. What they lack in tangible goods is balanced by an abundance of thankfulness. They acknowledge that what they do have are blessings from God.

If we embrace the gospel, we cannot sidestep poverty as something of value. We must hold our possessions lightly and practice detachment and generosity. In fact, if we embrace spiritual poverty, it will lead us to thanksgiving, generosity, and ultimately joy.

Points to Ponder

[Jesus] taught them, saying:

"Blessed are the poor in spirit, for theirs is the kingdom of heaven."

—Matthew 5:3

We want you to know, brethren, about the grace of God which has been shown in the churches of Macedonia, for in a severe test of affliction, their abundance of joy and their extreme poverty have overflowed in a wealth of liberality on their part. For they gave according to their means, as I can testify, and beyond their means, of their own free will, begging us earnestly for the favor of taking part in the relief of the saints.

—2 Corinthians 8:1–4

As for the rich in this world, charge them not to be haughty, nor to set their hopes on uncertain riches but on God who richly furnishes us with everything to enjoy. They are to do good, to be rich in good deeds, liberal and generous, thus laying up for themselves a good foundation for the future, so that they may take hold of the life which is life indeed.

—1 Timothy 6:17–19

Jesus enjoins his disciples to prefer him to everything and everyone, and bids them "renounce all that [they have]" for his sake and that of the Gospel. Shortly before his passion he gave them the example of the poor widow of Jerusalem who, out of her poverty, gave all that she had to live on. The precept of detachment from riches is obligatory for entrance into the Kingdom of heaven.

—*Catechism of the Catholic Church*, #2544;
Luke 14:33; see Mark 8:35

Prayer

Heavenly Father, no matter what my circumstances, help me to embrace spiritual poverty. I know that all I have is gift from you, and rather than possessing it, I am only a steward. I come now to you with an open heart and open hands, knowing that true wealth only comes from receiving what you give. No matter if it be lack or wealth, blessing or suffering, troubles or triumphs, I receive all as gift. Help me to exude the true thankfulness, generosity, and joy that come from being your child.

Discussion Questions and Action Steps

1. How is God challenging you to live spiritual poverty?
2. Make a list of items for which you should thank God and a list of items for which you should thank other people.
3. How does spiritual poverty lead to joy?

Where Is Your Heart?
::: On putting God first :::

Cindy is a wonderful Catholic woman with strong faith. Her commitment to the Lord and his Church is readily apparent in everything that she does. In her job as a social worker, it is obvious that her motivation in caring for children and families springs from her love of Christ.

Cindy and I share something: We are both bibliophiles—we like to buy, read, and keep books. I enjoy looking at all the books on my shelves, periodically taking one down, handling it, and rereading a passage or a few pages. I often joke that books are my one vice in life. I'm reluctant to give "my" books away. It's often a challenge just to lend a favorite book to someone.

It was while looking at the books on her shelves that God nudged Cindy. She was convinced that some of her books would be better off in the hands of someone else, rather than just sitting and collecting dust. It was not a revelation that gave her much comfort. Like me, she is attached to her books. It is a testament to her love of

God and commitment to following the promptings of the Holy Spirit that she said yes to his nudge. She decided that she would be open to giving texts from her library to others who would benefit from them.

Her decision that day didn't change her love of books. It didn't make it easy for her to part with them. In fact, each time she recognized that one of her books would benefit someone else, it required an active decision of the will to again say yes to God and part with the book.

I found out about this situation during conversation over dinner one evening. I don't remember the particular topic under discussion, but Cindy had a book on it that she felt would be helpful to me. With a gracious smile she offered to give that book to me. I only realized how much the book meant to her when I said that I already owned a copy, and Cindy gave a slight sigh of relief.

It was then that she told my wife and me about her decision to give books from her library to individuals who might be helped by them. She also admitted that it was difficult every time she did so. Each decision involved a dying to self in order to live for Christ and others. She also told us that sometimes God eased the pain of book separation by blessing her in some other way.

For example, there was one particular book that she struggled to give away. However, in the end she yielded to the prompting of the Holy Spirit. God's little blessing came shortly afterwards, when someone gave her another copy of the book she had given away! That might seem like a small blessing, but for Cindy it was a powerful witness of God's love for her. It was a sign that he honored her willingness to put everything in her life at his disposal.

When I give retreats during Lent, I often encourage my listeners to consider the Scripture from the Gospel of Matthew, "For where your treasure is, there will your heart be also" (6:21). It's important to ask the question, "What is my treasure?" We can identify our treasures by asking what it is that we believe we can't do without. For some it will be material—like books for Cindy and me. It might be money or a fancy car or designer clothes. It could be something less tangible, like power or prestige. We are not talking here about what is evil or bad. Often our treasure is something that in itself is good—a particular friend, our private time, and so on.

However, for a Catholic, God should be our treasure. Our heart is to be fixed on him. That doesn't mean that we must do without other goods, but it does mean that God and his will must be first in our lives.

If there is someone or something that I treasure more than Christ, I have a "heart" disorder that needs spiritual surgery. Only when I lay aside everything else to embrace Christ will my life be in good order.

As my friend Cindy found, God blesses those who embrace him and "seek first his kingdom and his righteousness" (Matthew 6:33). Of course, we don't put God first because we seek his gifts. Indeed, if we possess Christ, we possess everything, for he is Lord of all creation.

Points to Ponder

> Take delight in the LORD,
>> and he will give you the desires of your heart.
>
> —Psalm 37:4

Blessed is he who knows what it is to love Jesus and to despise himself for the sake of Christ. We must quit what we love for this Beloved, because Jesus will be loved alone above all things.... Love Him and keep Him for thy friend, who, when all go away, will not leave thee nor suffer thee to perish in the end. [1]

—Thomas à Kempis, *The Imitation of Christ*

Prayer

Heavenly Father, I know that you treasure me so much that you sent your only Son to die so that I might be saved. I desire that my heart would be fixed on you. Yet you know how I struggle with lesser loves that tug at my heart. I tell you now that you alone are my treasure. Help me to live out that decision every day of my life, so that when I die I will be ready to embrace you and rejoice in you alone. Amen.

Discussion Questions and Action Steps

1. Do some of your things actually possess you? What are they? What steps can you take to get free?

2. What nonmaterial possession has the strongest hold on your life? (Pleasure seeking? Power? Recognition? Other?) Is God calling you to change your perspective? How can you practically respond to God?

3. Do you have an excess of something, such as clothes, furniture, or other tangible items? Be open to giving from your excess to bless someone in their need.

Make a Memorial and Visit It Often
::: On an aid to prayer :::

The ancient Israelites had the curious custom of piling up rocks, often in the middle of nowhere, and of naming places and water wells with unusual titles. This building and naming was not a meaningless activity. Quite the opposite! These activities were charged with meaning. Here are some examples:

- When God promised to make Abraham's descendants as numerous "as the dust of the earth," Abraham erected an altar at the site (Genesis 13:14–18).
- When God stayed Abraham's hand before he killed Isaac and then provided a ram as an alternative sacrifice, Abraham named the place "The LORD will provide" (Genesis 22:14).
- Isaac built an altar where God had appeared to him and renewed the covenant God had made with his father Abraham (Genesis 26:23–25).

- In Genesis 28 the sacred author reports that Jacob saw angels ascending to and descending from heaven. Here Jacob set up a stone memorial pillar and renamed the place Bethel, which means "the house of God" (Genesis 28:10–22).
- See also Genesis 12:7 and Genesis 31:51–53.

Recall that the patriarchs and their extended families were nomads. They would move their flocks of sheep to good pasture lands and places where water was available. I can visualize Abraham, Isaac, and Jacob returning to the places where they had built altars, pillars, and memorials or where they had changed the name of the location. I'm sure that seeing these memorials again provided a witness and an opportunity to recall how God had worked in their lives.

The Church has long seen the value of the physical in helping us to reconnect with the spiritual. In my office, along with photos of my family, I have a crucifix and a statue of Mary. Whenever I raise my eyes from my computer screen, I see these two images. They remind me of who I am and what God has done in my life. I can take the opportunity to utter a short prayer or verbalize my commitment to God and his plan.

I spend considerable time at a computer screen, so I've used Scripture verses as the screen saver. At times I'll tape prayer intentions to the top of the screen as reminders to pray. I use the beads of the rosary to help me stay focused on the mysteries. My wife and I used to name our cars after saints.

We are nomads in this world. The markers and memorials that we place in our homes and at our places of work can help us concentrate on what is important. Then we will be less likely to be sidetracked in our journey to our goal—the beatific vision and eternal life in heaven.

Points to Ponder

"[Abraham] constructs an altar to the Lord at each stage of his journey."

—*Catechism of the Catholic Church*, #2570

Honorable and venerable images...we honor and salute.... So that through their representations we may be able to be led back in memory and recollection to the prototype, and have a share in the holiness of some one of them. [1]

—Second Council of Nicaea

I will go to the altar of God,
    to God my exceeding joy;
and I will praise you with the lyre,
    O God, my God.

—Psalm 43:4

Prayer

I give you praise, Lord, for as the psalmist writes, "so wonderfully you made me" (Psalm 139:14, *NAB*). I am a unique blend of body and spirit. I acknowledge that both are gift from you. Help me to use the physical as means of drawing closer to you, as a way to worship you, and as a reminder of "how precious to me are your designs, O God" (Psalm 139:17, *NAB*).

Discussion Questions and Action Steps

1. Do you pray at various times throughout the day? When? How?
2. What tangible items can you place in your home or office to remind you to turn to God in prayer throughout the day?
3. Man is unique, composed of body and soul. What is the relationship between the two? How can the material world help or hinder you in your spiritual life?

Alive in the Sky
::: On death and the Catholic faith :::

I worked as the director of Catholic cemeteries for three different dioceses: Pittsburgh, Tucson, and Boston. I didn't make a lot of money working for Catholic cemeteries, but I did get a lot of clothes! I had T-shirts from Pittsburgh, a jacket and a couple hats from Tucson, another jacket and various shirts from Boston. Instead of a kangaroo or a golf club on the breast pocket, much of my casual clothing had "Catholic Cemeteries" embroidered on it.

And I still wear these items regularly. You can't beat free clothing. But the words *cemeteries* and *Catholic* can elicit some interesting reactions from people. Once a hospital employee asked, "Do you really think it is appropriate to wear that in here?"

After many years of working for Catholic cemeteries, I began my own business as a consultant. I racked up quite a few frequent flyer miles traveling from city to city. Of course, I often wore my free cemetery clothing while flying.

On one particular flight there was a problem with the ticketing, and I was bumped up to first class. I found myself sitting next to a flight attendant who, having finished her routes for the day, was flying to where she would begin work the next day. I was wearing both a shirt and a jacket with the words *Catholic Cemeteries* embroidered on them.

I have the habit of trying to engage the person sitting next to me in a conversation—it often proves more interesting than the reading material I carry. Well, this young woman seemed to fulfill my stereotype of a flight attendant. She had a big smile and was very lively. She was sociable but restrained. Our conversation was pretty superficial until she chanced to notice my shirt. I could see her looking twice to be sure that she really saw "Catholic Cemeteries" written on it.

She said, "I can't help noticing your shirt. Do you work for a Catholic cemetery?" I gave her the brief version of my work history. To which she replied, "I don't practice now, but I was raised Catholic."

Since I didn't know exactly how to respond, there was a brief period of silence. Then tears began to form in the corners of her eyes, and with an unsteady voice she said, "My grandmother died three weeks ago."

Something had changed. The self-assured demeanor and the plastic smile were gone. As she cried she told me of her troubled childhood and of the love her Catholic grandmother had shown as the key caregiver in her young life. She described in detail the last earthly days of her grandmother's life and her grief at not being at her bedside when she passed on. She then told me about her present trials with her boyfriend and other difficulties in her life.

I mostly listened, asking a few questions and offering some affirming comments. When the time seemed right, I spoke to her about the fact that God had a plan for her life and that he was available to her. I encouraged her to pray and suggested that she may want to reexplore the faith of her childhood. She thanked me profusely. When we parted, and as she wiped away her tears, I promised to pray for her.

There Is a Need

This was neither the first nor the last conversation that I have had about death and the Catholic faith, perhaps because of the excessive time I spend on planes, where I have a captive audience! Also, my wife has told me that I have reached that age when I am the "non-threatening, father-figure type who has a good ear." And I think those two words on my shirt, *Catholic* and *cemeteries*, open doors—and hearts.

Every culture has its taboo subjects. Death and faith are two topics that you don't discuss in informal settings and casual meetings. It's not polite, or so we are told. People don't know how to respond. They get nervous, and the conversation gets difficult. Aren't we just expected to get over someone's death and move on?

It seems that the only time it is acceptable to grieve is when there has been some tragedy. People place flowers at the roadside where the accident happened or at the fence near the shooting site. However, the "normal" death of a mom or a grandpa we are supposed to handle differently. We can't wear our feelings on our sleeve. We have to maintain the decorum that is expected in polite company.

Yet the mystery of death and the centrality of faith pull at the heart and mind of every person. We can't escape the questions that they propose. Does death end my relationship with the deceased? Is there life after death? What is the importance of life? If there is no God and no afterlife, what is the meaning of life? Am I just a cosmic joke?

When I worked in Catholic cemeteries, I began to realize their value to people. Cemeteries are among the few places where it is OK to grieve. It is all right to talk to the deceased at the graveside and to release some of that pent-up emotion.

What about that other taboo topic, faith, and in particular, Catholic faith? It too is not terribly popular in our society. It seems that there are more Catholics who "used to go to church" than there are Catholics who do go to church. At least those are the people that I met most often on my flights.

I found that many of those nonpracticing Catholics maintain a certain identity as Catholic. There are still embers of faith that glow within them. Augustine was definitely right when he said that the soul cannot find rest until it rests in God.[1] There are many restless souls in our society. Knowing the interior struggles of so many people, I think it is worth being thought of as impolite, for a conversation on the Catholic faith and its answer to death can bring some hope and perspective and perhaps even change a life.

Points to Ponder

If Christ has not been raised, then our preaching is in vain and your faith is in vain....

But in fact Christ has been raised from the dead, the first fruits of those who have fallen asleep. For as by a man came death, by a man has come also the resurrection of the dead....

...Come to your right mind, and sin no more.

—1 Corinthians 15:14, 20–21, 34

We believe in the life eternal. We believe that the souls of all those who die in the grace of Christ—whether they must still be purified in purgatory, or whether from the moment they leave their bodies Jesus takes them to paradise as he did for the Good Thief—are the People of God in the eternity beyond death, which will be finally conquered on the day of the Resurrection when these souls will be reunited with their bodies. [2]

—Pope Paul VI, "The Credo of the People of God"

Prayer for Departed Loved Ones

Jesus, I know that the cords of love cannot be broken by death and the grave. I know that I am still united with my loved ones who have died, because we continue to share life in you. So I pray for the faithful departed.

Lord, in your mercy grant them eternal life and happiness in your heavenly home. Grant me the grace of faith and perseverance, so that I too may someday rejoice in your eternal presence. May it be so.

Discussion Questions and Action Steps

1. Do you fear death? Why or why not? What is a Catholic view of death?[3]
2. Reflect on a funeral you attended. Did the Church's liturgy help you? How so?
3. Read the *Catechism of the Catholic Church*, #958. Why are we encouraged to pray for the deceased?

Lenten Sacrifices
::: On overcoming bad habits :::

My morning routine in Tucson was pretty consistent. My youngest daughter, Beverly, and I would drive to Mass, and after Mass I would drop her off at school. So we spent thirty to forty minutes together every school day in the car. I have fond memories of our conversations during that time and of the growth in our relationship.

One year as we were approaching Lent, I asked Bev if she had decided what she was going to do for her lenten sacrifice. She hadn't decided, and when she asked the same question of me, I had to admit that neither had I. It was then that a Holy Spirit thought popped into my mind. "Why don't you come up with a lenten penance for me, and I will decide on one for you?" She readily agreed.

Later I spoke with my wife, asking her input on a good lenten sacrifice. She pointed out Beverly's predominate fault at that time. When asked to do something, Bev's response was initially almost always negative. Whether it was the directive to do homework, complete a task at the house, or go to bed, Bev's first response was to complain. She would ask, "Why me?" and display a mournful face. I agreed with Libbie. Attacking that bad habit and replacing it with a good habit would be a worthy lenten project. About a week later Bev and I were in the car on our morning itinerary, and I broached the lenten discussion again.

"Bev, have you thought any more about Lent?"

"Yes, I think I'll give up candy and gum."

"That's good," I said, "but there may be a better lenten penance for you."

I then reviewed her problem of an unhelpful attitude and suggested the alternative lenten sacrifice that my wife and I had discussed. The look in her eyes and her body language betrayed her struggle with this suggestion. She listened as I further described the proposal.

"Bev, I suggest that whenever you want to complain, you instead thank God for something. I'll help you. Whenever I see that you are starting to complain, I'll tug on my earlobe. That will give you the clue to catch yourself and say thank you rather than something negative."

After staring at me in some disbelief for a moment, she responded, "But, Dad, that's hard!"

"Honey, yes, it will be hard, but don't you think Jesus would be pleased if you tried to overcome this fault?"

"Yes."

"Don't you think it would be more pleasing to him than giving up gum and candy?"

"Well, yes."

As I pulled on my earlobe, I said, "Let's give it a try."

There wasn't much enthusiasm, but she did agree.

I then asked the million-dollar question: "Bev, have you thought about what I should do for Lent?" A parent should be smarter than to put that decision into the hands of a nine-year-old, but I've never been very bright.

Before I tell you the instructions that Beverly gave me, I need to give you a little background. It goes without saying that it is hot in Tucson. The regular intake of fluids is important. My drink of choice was diet cola—no sugar but plenty of caffeine. Every day I would drink a "Big Gulp," probably two liters of diet cola. It not only quenched my thirst but also helped with frequent headaches to which I was prone (probably due to all that caffeine!).

Well, you can probably guess what Beverly thought was a good lenten penance for me. "Dad, I think you should give up soda for Lent."

"But, Bev," I said, "cola helps me with my headaches, and it's a great thirst quencher, and..."

She interrupted me in the middle of my excuses. "Dad, mine's hard."

I was stuck. Of course, she was right. I was left no choice. I had to give up cola.

I think the withdrawal period was three days. It was not easy. I had headaches, and I was irritable. Bev probably handled her lenten penance better than I did mine, at least initially.

That daily cola was arguably a small vice from the perspective of my entire spiritual life, but there is no doubt that God wanted and wants all of me. He wants each of us to submit everything to him. After all, his call is that we be perfect. Jesus tells his disciples, "You, therefore, must be perfect, as your heavenly Father is perfect" (Matthew 5:48). He wants to be fully Lord over every area of our lives.

Have no doubt—that is not an easy process for the fallen nature of man. It is a lifelong struggle. We must not become discouraged; rather each and every day we must renew the struggle. Overcoming bad habits and the sinfulness that underlies them is an important goal. Yet the very process of overcoming our faults, which involves regular examinations of conscience, repentance, trust in God, and the necessary decisions to continue the struggle, is also important—perhaps even more important than the goal itself. Progress is a result of both God's grace and our response. The entire journey of this life is time to submit all to God and deepen our relationship with him. Not easy, but the rewards are divine!

Points to Ponder

> Brethren, I do not consider that I have made it my own; but one thing I do, forgetting what lies behind and straining forward to what lies ahead, I press on toward the goal for the prize of the upward call of God in Christ Jesus.
>
> —Philippians 3:13–14

> Certainly our goal is both lofty and difficult to attain. But please do not forget that people are not born holy. Holiness is forged through a constant interplay of God's grace and the correspondence of man. [1]
>
> —St. Josemaría Escrivá, *Friends of God*

Prayer

Lord, you and I both know the bad habit with which I continue to struggle. You know how weak I am. Yet I embrace the hope that I have in you. I believe that all is possible by your grace. I now recommit myself to the struggle. I now begin anew. Grant me the strength to persevere.

My guardian angel, my patron saint, intercede for me.

Discussion Questions and Action Steps

1. What is the bad habit with which you most struggle? What virtue do you need to foster in order to help you overcome that habit?
2. What can you do to cooperate with God's grace in this area? What is your battle plan for this struggle? (Regular confession? Accountability to someone? Avoiding temptation? Fasting? Other?)
3. Why does the Church encourage penitential practices, especially during Lent? (For help with this question, see "Lent" in the Glossary of the *Catechism* and the following sections: 540, 1095, and 1438.)

Fluffy Towels

::: On showing honor :::

While shopping my wife noticed that the expensive towels were on sale. You know the type–the comfortable ones with the fluffy pile that feels good on the skin. Anyway, she bought a bath towel and a matching washcloth. After an initial washing, she placed them on top of the other towels in the linen closet. You couldn't miss them. They were at least twice as thick as any other set in the closet.

However, I began to think that they were invisible to my wife. Every time I went to the closet, they were sitting on top of all those other towels. They were never used. Of course, when I took a towel set, I'd lift the new towel and washcloth with one hand and take the set underneath for my use. You see, I wanted my wife to have the benefit of the comfort they offered. But the set was always there the next time I'd go to get a towel.

Eventually I said to Libbie, "Why haven't you used the new towel?"

Her response: "I've been taking a different set so that you will have the new towel. How come you haven't used it?"

"I wanted you to use it, so I've been taking the second set each time!" I replied.

Laughing, we continued the "argument" about who would use the towel and who would be self-sacrificial and bypass it. I eventually "gave in" and inaugurated it with a first use.

When told the story, our children said that we were a "cute" old couple.

A Healthy Competition

Scripture tells us that we are to "outdo one another in showing honor" (Romans 12:10). This is the competition that strengthens the bonds of love, whether between spouses, parent and child, or friends.

In marriage we are called to lay down our lives for one another, just as Christ offered his life on the cross for our salvation. That is quite a challenge, both in magnitude of sacrifice and in the ongoing nature of the call. Indeed, we need to find ways to daily show that love to our spouse. Showing honor is a way to love primarily through the little things.

Social conventions used to dictate that a man would hold the door for his wife and let her go first. That practice has almost disappeared in our society, but it had a value. It was a way of saying, "I love you enough that I willingly inconvenience myself for you. I honor you and see your value, and I am willing to sacrifice for you."

Actions such as turning off the television to talk with your spouse, making the dinner your spouse enjoys even though you don't like it, getting up with the baby even though it's not your turn, waiting to start eating (and keeping the kids from starting to eat) until your spouse is seated and ready to begin are all little ways of dying to self for the sake of the beloved. The possibilities are only limited by our imaginations.

Sometime ago I read a book on World War I. The author told of a general who explained to a soldier why he was so demanding about little things—having shoes spit polished, doing drills with precision, having the bed made just right, saluting with exactitude, and so on. He demanded this strict regime so that in the heat of combat, the soldier would act appropriately—with precision, with obedience, with courage.

Christ tells us that we are to be ready to lay down our lives for our spouse—to literally take the bullet if necessary. Most of us won't be called to that form of giving our life. However, we will be called in other ways. We must be prepared to resist temptation and exercise virtue that can be heroic when our spouse is sick, when we face financial difficulties or job loss, when death touches our lives, when our children go astray or suffer difficulty, when we must bypass some opportunity for the sake of our family, when a spouse sins against us. If we are to love in those situations as Christ has loved us, we must be well practiced in the art of love. That is why daily small acts of love and honor are so important. They prepare us for the bigger tests.

There is no person on earth who sees and knows my faults more clearly than my wife. Yet there is no one who speaks more of my virtues and honors me more by her actions than Libbie. People see me as a balding old guy. She chooses to see beyond the physical, recognize her beloved groom, and honor him in ways that are truly godlike.

To consistently honor one another—whether spouse, parent, friend, or even enemy—by our words and deeds is truly to be like Christ. It is also great training for the greater challenges of life. It is preparation to follow the example of Jesus, no matter to what we may be called—even if we are called to take the bullet.

Points to Ponder

So if there is any encouragement in Christ, any incentive of love, any participation in the Spirit, any affection and sympathy, complete my joy by being of the same mind, having the same love, being in full accord and of one mind. Do nothing from selfishness or conceit, but in humility count others better than yourselves. Let each of you look not only to his own interests, but also to the interests of others.

—Philippians 2:1–4

Remind them...to speak evil of no one, to avoid quarreling, to be gentle, and to show perfect courtesy toward all men.

—Titus 3:1–2

Love is...a journey, an ongoing exodus out of the closed inward-looking self towards its liberation through self-giving, and thus towards authentic self-discovery and indeed the discovery of God: "Whoever seeks to gain his life will lose it, but whoever loses his life will preserve it" (Luke 17:33).[1]

—Pope Benedict XVI, *Deus Caritas Est*

Prayer

How you have blessed me, Lord, with my family and friends! I desire to love them with the love with which you love them—a pure and unselfish love. Open my eyes to see opportunities when I can serve and honor them, and give me the grace to seize those opportunities.

I want to love in practical, tangible ways—big and small. It's easy for me to think of self first, but I want to develop the habit of thinking of the other's well-being before my own. I truly desire to love my family and friends, not only when they are lovable but always.

I know I can do it with your help. Thank you, Jesus!

Discussion Questions and Action Steps

1. How well are you doing in the "competition" of showing honor?
2. List three things that you could do to honor your spouse, parent, or friend.
3. Read again the quote from Pope Benedict XVI in the "Points to Ponder." How is self-giving liberating? How does it help us discover God?

God's on the Phone
::: On cooperating with God's work :::

When I was younger I would answer the telephone at home by saying, "Hello. Praise the Lord! This is Rege." This greeting elicited a variety of responses from the other end of the line. Sometimes there was silence. On one occasion the caller responded with "Well, pass the ammunition."

There was a call one evening that was definitely more memorable than any other. After I answered the phone with my normal greeting, there was a moment of silence, and then the caller said, "I think I have the wrong number." We verified that he had dialed incorrectly. Before I hung up the phone, I said, "God bless."

A minute later the telephone rang again. I answered, "Hello. Praise the Lord! This is Rege."

It was the same man. "Hi, I just called a minute ago. Are you a Christian?" I responded affirmatively. He continued, "I'm in a lot of trouble. Can we talk?"

He then explained that he had been arrested for theft and was out of jail on bail. When he accidentally got me on the telephone, he had been trying to call someone to make final arrangements to flee the area rather than face prosecution. Although determined to do this, he had been feeling somewhat uneasy about the prospect. Then he got the wrong number!

We talked. I prayed with him and promised continuing prayer. He told me that he would make his court appearance. He ended the conversation with the comment "I don't think getting you as a wrong number was an accident." I breathed a silent *Amen*.

The success of that conversation was due to the grace of God and the work of the Holy Spirit. A man needed to make the right decision, and God was ready and willing to help him. Perhaps his mother or some friend had been praying for him; perhaps even he had asked for God's help. I was available, and God worked through me. Indeed, praise God!

But I want to testify that the phone call also helped me. At the time I had been discouraged by the seeming fruitlessness of my efforts as an evangelist. The conversation reenergized me and taught me a lesson that I still need to have reinforced to this day.

Evangelism and conversion are works of God. The Holy Spirit is the one who changes people's hearts. Grace is the operative element. We are instruments. We can be conduits through which grace can flow to others, if we make ourselves available.

This fact both sets us free and fills us with awe. It sets us free because we realize that everything does not depend on us. When we are successful, we thank God that his work is moving forward. When we seem to fail, despite our best efforts, we recall that each person has free will and that God forces no one to come to him.

Don't get me wrong. Complacency isn't the answer. The fact that he chooses to work through us should incite us to greater faithfulness.

Signs and wonders were often evident in the lives of the saints. Their apostolates frequently were very effective, although not always. The results were the work of God, but the saints had become such pure channels that grace rushed with little hindrance to those whom God wished to reach. God can use any vessel as a means of reaching out to people. Yet there is no doubt that those who are closest to God are often the best channels of his grace.

Let us always remember that our apostolate is contingent on the work of God. It is only as we draw ever closer to the source of grace that it will flow through us effectively to bless others.

Points to Ponder

I charge you in the presence of God and of Christ Jesus who is to judge the living and the dead, and by his appearing and his kingdom: preach the word, be urgent in season and out of season, convince, rebuke, and exhort, be unfailing in patience and in teaching.... Always be steady, endure suffering, do the work of an evangelist, fulfil your ministry.

—2 Timothy 4:1–2, 5

"Christ…is the source of the Church's whole apostolate"; thus the fruitfulness of apostolate for ordained ministers as well as for lay people clearly depends on their vital union with Christ [*Apostolicam actuositatem*, 4; see John 15:5]. In keeping with their vocations, the demands of the times and the various gifts of the Holy Spirit, the apostolate assumes the most varied forms.

—*Catechism of the Catholic Church*, #864

Prayer

Lord, it is when I am close to you that I find salvation, peace, joy, and all that is good. I desire to bring others to you, so that they too may enjoy the blessing and hope that come from a relationship with you. Thank you, Lord, that you deign to work through me to bless others.

I know that I am a sinner and therefore an imperfect example and conduit of your grace. I repent of my sin and ask that you would draw me closer to you. And through my closeness to you, may others be drawn into the family of God.

Discussion Questions and Action Steps

1. Do you know someone who is facing a difficult decision? Is there a way that you could help that person in his or her decision making?

2. Have you experienced being an agent of the Holy Spirit? What happened?

3. Is your faith evident by what you say? Is there more you can do to point to God in your conversations? Explain.

I Am Guilty

::: On personal sin :::

It's reported that G.K. Chesterton once responded to an article in the *London Times* on the theme "What is wrong with the world?" Chesterton responded: "Dear Sirs: I am."

There are many problems and wrongs in the world and in the Church. We can discuss them and theorize on solutions. However, the most effective means of addressing what is wrong in the world is personal conversion, which is an ongoing process.

At a parish where my family worshiped years ago, there was an older Catholic woman whom I would describe as eccentric. She dressed oddly. When she came into church, she wouldn't just genuflect; she would get down on both knees, bend forward, and kiss the floor. She would spend an inordinate amount of time in front of the statue of the Blessed Mother. She went to Mass twice each day.

One Saturday I was in line for confession, and this woman was in the same line with a young woman. I must tell you that the young woman looked like a prostitute. She certainly didn't appear to be your average churchgoer. Her hair was a shade of purple, and her clothing was less than modest. The older Catholic woman was talking to her and encouraging her.

Eventually the young woman's turn came, and she went into the confessional. She was there for a long time. I was impatiently waiting and getting irritated. I had things to do!

Finally the woman came out with tears rolling down her face and with the biggest smile imaginable. She and the older woman exchanged a big hug. It was only then that I realized my sin.

While a young woman was being saved, healed, and cleansed in the sacrament of reconciliation, I was impatiently waiting in line, wishing she would hurry up so that I could get on with my day. I can't remember what tasks were so "important" to me. However, I imagine that woman will not forget her experience of that day.

Pharisaism

The Pharisees were the religious folk in the days of Jesus. They kept all of the precepts of the Law. They were the "church people" that others would seek to emulate. Yet Jesus said to them, "Woe to you, scribes and Pharisees, hypocrites! for you are like whitewashed tombs, which outwardly appear beautiful, but within they are full of dead men's bones and all uncleanness" (Matthew 23:27). Quite a stinging condemnation from the lips of meek and merciful Jesus!

I am among the religious folk of today. I keep the rules. You will frequently find me at church or involved in Catholic activities. Others look to me as an example to emulate. If transported back two thousand years, I wouldn't feel uncomfortable among the Pharisees.

On that day while I waited impatiently for confession, Jesus could have appropriately spoken to me as he had addressed those Pharisees. I was a hypocrite. Outwardly I appeared righteous, but inwardly there was "iniquity." I didn't hear the "dead men's bones" rattling within me until I saw tears of grateful joy rolling down the cheeks of two women.

I hope that incident is the exception in my life and not the rule. If otherwise, I hope to be addressed as a "whitewashed tomb" so that I can again repent.

I assume that most people who read this essay are also among the religious folk. I hope you display all that is good in being known as such. Yet since we are religious, we are all prone to pharisaism. Chesterton saw it clearly. What is wrong with the world? I am. We are. We need continuing conversion to get our priorities right, embrace the faith fully, and adopt God's perspective. We need to be saved from not only our sins of commission but also our sins of omission, our complacency and self-righteousness.

Am I wrong to ask you and me to focus on our sinfulness when we already do so much that is right and godly? No, because there is a great blessing in recognizing our sins. When we do, we can also recognize our need for the Savior. We are indeed foolish if we rely on our own self-righteousness. We are indeed truly blessed when we recognize our failures and shortcomings and then turn and are captured in the embrace of the heavenly Father who receives back the prodigal.

Sin is the greatest horror of human existence, yet the Easter *Exultet* proclaims, *O felix culpa quae talem et tantum meruit habere redemptorem* ("O happy fault that merited such and so great a Redeemer").

Our call is not merely to be religious; we are to be perfect, as Christ is perfect. We are to grow into the fullness of his stature (see Ephesians 4:13). This is the work of a lifetime and, for many of us, will include a bit of purgatory before we are ready for the beatific vision.

Points to Ponder

If we say we have no sin, we deceive ourselves, and the truth is not in us. If we confess our sins, he is faithful and just, and will forgive our sins and cleanse us from all unrighteousness. If we say we have not sinned, we make him a liar, and his word is not in us.

—1 John 1:8–10

The words and deeds of Jesus and those of his Church are not meant only for those who are sick or suffering or in some way neglected by society. On a deeper level they affect the very meaning of every person's life in its moral and spiritual dimensions. Only those who recognize that their life is marked by the evil of sin can discover in an encounter with Jesus the Savior the truth and the authenticity of their own existence. Jesus himself says as much: "Those who are well have no need of a physician, but those who are sick; I have not come to call the righteous, but sinners to repentance" (Luke 5:31–32).[1]

—Blessed Pope John Paul II, *Evangelium Vitae*

Prayer

Lord, save me from the self-righteousness to which I am prone. Let me have a sober judgment of my sinfulness, so that I not fall into the trap of pharisaism. Lord, when I examine my conscience, open my eyes to see where I fall short of the call you have on my life. Then let me repent and focus not so much upon my sin but upon the embrace of the Father and upon the grace that flows from you and gives me new strength.

Jesus, give me your heart, your perspective, and your ability to love. Amen.

Discussion Questions and Action Steps

1. At the beginning of each Mass is the Penitential Rite. Do you use this time to truly recall your sins and ask God's forgiveness?

2. How can you guard against pharisaism in your life?

3. Do you take responsibility for personal sin? Do you daily examine your conscience and regularly go to confession?

A Clean Refrigerator
::: On humble service :::

It was the first day of my employment as the executive director of a cemetery organization. I went to place my lunch in the refrigerator in the employee cafeteria. It was immediately obvious that it had not been cleaned for a long time. There were various shades of mold on the different foods, spilled beverages, and a broken mustard bottle.

My inquiries turned up the fact that cleaning the office refrigerator was no one's responsibility. I quickly concluded that it must then be everyone's responsibility. Since I intended to use the refrigerator, it seemed appropriate that it be my turn to clean it.

On the subsequent Saturday I brought one of my children with me to work, with the promise of a free lunch for helping Dad with a "little project." We cleaned and defrosted the refrigerator and then enjoyed lunch together. Work accomplished and one-on-one time with one of my children was a winning combination as far as I was concerned.

What I did not expect was the reaction of my fellow employees on Monday morning. Word quickly spread that the new director had cleaned the refrigerator. Some of my coworkers apologized; others remonstrated that I shouldn't be doing that work. After all, I was the director.

My answer for all was the same: "It needed to be done, so I did it." For the next five years I had to fight to get the opportunity to clean that refrigerator, because it truly became everyone's job!

I've always believed that no job is "beneath my dignity." Jesus is our example. He bent down to serve us by becoming man and suffering and dying for us.

When we serve others, in imitation of Jesus, we truly serve him. St. Thérèse of Lisieux, the Little Flower, lived and taught a spirituality founded on doing small things with great love. She compared it to a small child's scattering fragrant flowers. Heroism is found not only in doing great deeds but also in doing small things with great love.

Points to Ponder

Let no one seek his own good, but the good of his neighbor, ... just as I try to please all men in everything I do, not seeking my own advantage, but that of many, that they may be saved.

—1 Corinthians 10: 24, 33

Love needs to be proved by action. Well, even a little child can scatter flowers, to scent the throne-room with their fragrance.... That shall be my life, to scatter flowers, here by a smiling look, there by a kind word, always doing the tiniest things right, and doing it for love.[1]

—St. Thérèse of Lisieux, *Autobiography*

Prayer

Dear Lord, you never tell us to do what is impossible, and yet you can see more clearly than I do how weak and imperfect I am; if, then, you tell me to love my [neighbors] as you love them, that must mean that you yourself go on loving them in and through me—you know it wouldn't be possible in any other way. There would have been no new commandment, if you hadn't meant to give me the grace to keep it; how I welcome it, then, as proof that your will is to love, in and through me, all the people you tell me to love! [2]

—St. Thérèse of Lisieux, *Autobiography*

Discussion Questions and Action Steps

1. Reread the quote from St. Thérèse of Lisieux in "Points to Ponder." How could you improve in putting love into action?
2. Read the parable of the talents in Matthew 25:14–30. God is looking for "good and faithful servants." How well are you responding to this call? Where can you improve?
3. How well does your life reflect St. Paul's words, "I bid every one among you not to think of himself more highly than he ought to think, but to think with sober judgment" (Romans 12:3)?

Personalized Care

::: On care for the poor :::

If you have lived in or visited the desert Southwest, you probably know that there are many people who live there only seasonally. Retirees will winter there, and people with financial means will have their second home there. Others come with the hope of finding employment in the winter. A final group who winter there are people who live on the streets and keep body and soul together by begging.

When I was the director of Catholic Cemeteries in Tucson, Roger was the foreman of the maintenance crew at the largest cemetery. He was also the father of a large family that included both biological and adopted children. He was a solid Catholic whose faith coursed through him from his head to the soles of his feet. He would have struggled to give a definition of *transubstantiation*, although I'm sure he believed in it passionately because the Church taught it. But his faith was most evident not in his words but in his deeds.

Roger believed in giving people chances. He had worked as a probation officer before working at the cemeteries. So he first convinced me to allow people who needed to do community service as part of a court sentence to do that service at the cemetery. Roger would take them under his wing.

Roger next told me how difficult it was for those just coming out of prison to find their first job. So we began keeping one laborer's position open just for recently released prisoners. They were paid only slightly more than the minimum wage, but this first job gave them a platform from which to find their second. We also, at various times, had young recovering drug addicts working at the cemetery, often providing them with their first experience of work—at least work that was legal.

I wasn't really surprised when Roger came and told me that he wanted to give a job to a street beggar. Tim (not his real name) was a Vietnam veteran who had brought his family to Tucson in hopes of finding a job and because the weather would allow them to continue to live in their ancient and dilapidated mobile home. Tim had been standing at a busy entrance ramp to a highway holding a sign, "I'll work for food," when a passing driver told him, "Go to Catholic Cemeteries. They give anybody a job."

We never found out who told Tim to come to us, whether it was a man or an angel, or whether he did it to mock Tim or to help him. That, however, isn't important. Tim came to the cemetery and asked for work—at first just for what his sign requested, for food. Thus Roger was asking me to give him a job.

I looked out the window at Tim, and he looked like what you would expect of a street beggar. I must admit I was more than a little reluctant, but Roger convinced me that this might be the work of the Holy Spirit. He asked me to "give him a chance," even if it was only for a week. So we hired Tim. That action was the beginning of one of the greatest transformations that I have ever witnessed.

Tim parked his mobile home on a corner of the property and ran a hose to the vehicle for water. Roger got him some clothes, and we helped him get some food. Tim had challenges at work. He was quick-tempered and could be irritable with his coworkers. But Roger practiced some tough love and corrected Tim when needed.

Under Roger's tutelage Tim improved, and we decided to move him from a minimum-wage position to one with a regular worker's pay. This gave Tim enough money to rent a modest apartment within walking distance of work. Roger provided the security deposit.

Tim was then able to get his daughter enrolled in school. Over time Roger helped him get counseling and other help through Catholic Charities. Tim and his family also returned to Church—the initial trips were with Roger's family and at Roger's invitation.

Tim blossomed. He still struggled at times with anger, but he was gaining better control, and he showed himself to be a hard worker.

After Tim had worked at the cemetery for months, Roger encouraged him to look for other, better-paying employment. I will always remember the day that Tim walked into my office with Roger to tell me that he had been offered a better job. I congratulated Tim, but he had a question. "Is it OK if I leave, because I got this new job offer only because of what Roger and you have done for me? I'm really grateful, and if you want me to stay, I will."

Tim was loyal, and he valued what he had found with us. I told him that we were delighted that he was offered a better job and that we would support him in any way we could. It was then that this Vietnam veteran began to cry, and Roger and I had to fight to hold back our own tears.

Tim did leave us for that better-paying job, and the last I heard he was doing quite well. Roger would never take credit for Tim's transformation; he would give credit to God. And surely it was God's work, but the miracle came through the heart and hands of Roger.

In our epoch in history, most charity comes through a pen and a checkbook. Yet Jesus presents charity as a personal encounter with those in need. We are to go the extra mile for the person who asks us for one mile (see Matthew 5:41). The Good Samaritan didn't call the health department to help an injured man; he cared for him personally (Luke 10:33–35). Jesus touched the untouchable leper (Matthew 8:2–3).

We should continue to send our money to charities while not neglecting the more personal opportunities to touch our neighbor with God's love. You probably already are thinking of someone who needs your help. Step out and do it. As Roger told me, "It just might be the Holy Spirit."

Points to Ponder

Give to the one who asks of you, and do not turn your back on one who wants to borrow.

—Matthew 5:42, *NAB*

You received without pay, give without pay.

—Matthew 10:8b

God blesses those who come to the aid of the poor and rebukes those who turn away from them…. It is by what they have done for the poor that Jesus Christ will recognize his chosen.

—*Catechism of the Catholic Church*, #2443;
see Matthew 25:31–36

Prayer

Jesus, open my eyes to see the poverty, whether physical, spiritual, or emotional, that is around me—at work, in my community, in my social network, and in my family. Help me to share what you have graciously given to me with those I encounter. Especially help me to share your love in practical ways.

Discussion Questions and Action Steps

1. Read Matthew 25:34–40. Who is Jesus instructing you to serve?
2. When you meet a street beggar, what is your approach? Why?
3. What social outreach (for example, St. Vincent DePaul Society, food bank, crisis pregnancy help) does your parish do? Is there a way that you can help in that work or support it?

A Catholic Warrior

::: On living a humble and holy life :::

My maternal grandmother, Lavina, the oldest of ten children born to John and Annie Musher, was the keeper of the family history and stories. I heard many family tales at my grandmother's kitchen table, with a warm drink in one hand and a donut in the other. She was a master at telling a tale and extrapolating a lesson. She often held us spellbound or caused us to burst into laughter. She is a primary inspiration for this book that you hold in your hands.

Every cell in Lavina's body was Catholic. She unabashedly loved God and the faith. She opened my eyes to the heroism and virtue that was to be found so close at hand—in my extended family.

Lavina lived to be a hundred years old, and she maintained her mental capacity until the end. Although her formal education ended at eighth grade, she had a keen intellect. In addition to her amazing memory and skills as a storyteller, she loved to read. She often said that she would never complain about her health as long as her eyesight was good. She regularly thanked God for her good vision and the opportunity to read.

She also remained current on the news. At the age of ninety-six, she could still tell me the scores from the previous day's baseball game and expound on what the team needed to do to improve.

But I will most remember my grandmother as a woman of prayer. She had a prayer book that was well-worn from years of daily use. Held together with a rubber band, its tattered pages contained prayer cards from the funerals of the many people in her life who had died. She prayed daily for the living and for the faithful departed. I am sure many souls were freed from purgatory due to her prayers and sacrifices on their behalf.

The rosary was her constant companion. Whenever one of her granddaughters or granddaughters-in-law was pregnant, she would say a daily rosary for her and for the baby in the womb. With her large family that could involve many daily rosaries—one for each expectant mother. She prayed my four children safely into this world.

Lavina's travels were limited. She spent most of her life on the north side of Pittsburgh—in fact, in the family home on Goe Avenue. There she had given birth to her children, encouraged her husband, cared for her aging mother, and provided hospitality to many relatives and friends. She truly made a house into a home that radiated love and support. The center of life in that home was the kitchen table. World crises and family trials and joys were shared there—with a kettle of water boiling on the stove for a cup of tea or cocoa.

In her later years my grandmother was limited physically. I remember her hobbling about on legs terribly disfigured and bowed from arthritis. She went from a cane to a walker and eventually to a wheelchair. Yet I can't remember her complaining. To the question of "How are you feeling, Grandma?" she would inevitably respond,

"Oh, fine." She would then move the conversation to a topic more important to her, perhaps what I was doing at school. Her concern was always other focused. She was a good listener—perhaps that was the source of her skills as a storyteller.

Although bound to her home for many years of her later life, she had a ministry that reached far and wide. People would regularly call her, knowing that in Lavina they would find a sympathetic ear and someone who would help in bearing concerns. It seemed that everyone told his or her troubles to my grandmother.

She was in many ways ageless. She would tell me of "that poor old man" who lived up the street. That "poor old man" may have been seventy years old, while my grandmother was well into her eighties. She never saw herself as elderly. And she could relate to people young and old with ease and grace.

At the age of eighty-seven, she suffered a stroke. Having given birth to her children at home, this was her first time being a patient in a hospital. Nurses came to her room to marvel at the woman who at eighty-seven was in the hospital for the first time.

The death of her only son was a severe blow, causing this normally peaceful woman to display some anger. She told me that it was the most difficult event in her entire life and that she didn't know what to do. With the brashness of my youth, I told her that God was asking her to say yes one more time. She did not resent my comment, and indeed, she again said yes.

Once she passed the age of ninety years, she started to talk about the party she planned for her hundredth birthday, even as her health began to fail. Her kidney function was limited, and she had to be hospitalized a couple times and placed on intravenous fluids to deal with water retention. Yet she remained forward looking. Her goal was that celebration when she reached the age of a hundred.

The family rented a hall for a buffet dinner. A long line of friends and relatives filed in to wish Lavina a happy birthday. Seated in her wheelchair, she reigned like a queen. She immediately remembered most of those who greeted her; for a few she needed a reminder to place the face with a name. But with everyone she shared a story of their past dealings with one another. She loved people and could share something special and meaningful with each one. It was indeed a glorious day of celebration.

After the party her health declined considerably. The long-anticipated goal had been reached, and she began preparing for her death. She had been living with my mother, her daughter, during this time. It became apparent that my mother could no longer care for her, because Grandma had lost the strength to get out of the wheelchair.

Grandma agreed to be placed in a nursing home. She asked that it be a Catholic home, with a chapel where she could attend Mass and pray. The arrangements were made, and Grandma moved.

It was on her second day at the home, while my mother was visiting, that Lavina asked to be wheeled to the chapel for a visit. My mother took her there for a short period of prayer. Lavina then told her daughter that she was tired and wanted to take a nap. My mother took her back to the room and bid farewell. It was a final farewell, because before my mother had completed the drive home, Lavina passed from this world to the next.

Grandma knew her share of trials and hardships in her hundred years of life. She seldom complained and generally kept her focus on prayer and care for others. Until the end she remained a woman of faith and an example of goodness and love.

Points to Ponder

The wisdom of a humble man will lift up his head,
and will seat him among the great.

—Sirach 11:1

The prayer of the humble pierces the clouds.

—Sirach 35:17

In our Creed we confess that the Church herself is "holy." Not that we think everyone in the Church is holy. Not that everything in her is good, but in the sense that she is touched by the Lord and saints are forever growing within her. It is important that we should take the concept of holiness in a sufficiently broad sense, for there, too, there is no uniformity. And when the figures of the saints come before us, we can see how many shapes and fashions of sanctity there are. From a doctor who does his work unselfishly, to a scholar, to simple folk, founders of religious orders, and lay people who live their lives in this world.

What is important for me is to see the many inconspicuous saints, simple people like the ones I got to know in my childhood, like kind old farmers, kind dutiful mothers, who have given up their lives for their children, for their family, for the Church, and always for the other people in the village as well. It really doesn't have to have anything of the heroic about it, no, it can just be a matter of simple and humble things. [1]

—Cardinal Joseph Ratzinger [Pope Benedict XVI],
God and the World

Prayer

If my grandmother were still here, she would suggest that we say the prayer that both honors and asks the intercession of the greatest yet most humble woman ever born, Mary, the Lord's mother and ours as well. I can suggest nothing better.

Hail Mary,
full of grace,
the Lord is with thee.
Blessed art thou among women,
and blessed is the fruit
of thy womb, Jesus.
Holy Mary,
Mother of God,
pray for us sinners
now and at the hour of our death.
Amen.

Discussion Questions and Action Steps

1. Who in your family has been an inspiration to you? In what ways? If that person is still living, let him or her know how he or she has inspired you!

2. What are the qualities of a humble person?

3. Consider the humility, strength, and obedience of the Virgin Mary. Ask for her help to grow in virtue.

The Christmas Spirits
::: On living our faith in the workplace :::

When I was much younger—my three oldest children were still quite young—I worked for an electric utility company. I had taken the job simply because it was available, and with overtime we could make it financially. I saw it as a stopgap until the "right" position came along. If I ever underestimated the value of a job, I underestimated this one.

The power generation plant where I worked was hot and dirty. Coal dust was in the air, and the noise from the furnace, conveyors, and generators was constant. Employees wore dust masks and hearing protection.

My primary responsibility was to keep the bathrooms clean. Cleaning toilets was not work for which I would have volunteered, and it hadn't been in my college curriculum. However, I soon found that my tasks kept my hands busy and left my mind free, giving me ample opportunity to pray and reflect. As I worked and prayed, I experienced a closeness to Our Lord that I had never experienced in the office setting where I had worked previously.

I also quickly discovered that employees at the power station had been constantly grumbling about the condition of the bathrooms. My predecessors had not been very conscientious about cleaning. I decided that I would provide the cleanest bathrooms that my coworkers had ever seen. Now, I admit that I didn't receive many accolades for my labor. Nonetheless, every day I went home with a sense of satisfaction. I could see results from my efforts. I knew I was serving others and making their work environment just a little more pleasant.

I also got to know the other eleven janitors at the plant. We had our own break room, where we shared lunch. They could be a crude group, passing around *Playboy* and other such magazines. They soon realized that I wanted no part of pornographic literature. I would read from my pocket New Testament after lunch. My coworkers started to call me "Father" because of my Catholic beliefs. Mostly it was good-natured kidding, except when it came from a coworker I'll call Ed. He seemed to take delight in tormenting me because of my faith.

"I'd tell you a joke, but 'Father' is in the room," he would say. "Why don't we let 'Father Rege,' see the magazine? Oh, I forgot. He's religious."

These were typical of Ed's remarks. I would ignore them or just smile in response. I did one other thing: I started to pray regularly for Ed.

On Christmas Eve the janitors held a small party in the break room. Everyone brought food, and someone brought beer. Ed was the one who overindulged. He roared and sang and made me the butt of his jokes. Then suddenly he turned and walked over to me. When he stuck his finger in my chest, I expected the worst.

Instead Ed said, "Father, you are the only real man here! I used to be a Catholic, but I never go to church anymore. But you—you live what you believe. I wish I was like you." He then began to cry. Not only had the alcoholic spirits affected Ed but also the Holy Spirit. In the days that followed, Ed and I talked seriously about our Catholic faith. He agreed to see a priest, and I made the introduction and helped set up the first appointment. He returned to the sacraments and began to read good Catholic literature, which I readily supplied. Soon there were two of us who could be found reading the Bible at lunch.

I eventually returned to office work that was cleaner, less noisy, and better paying and had opportunities for advancement. But I left my work at the utility company with more than a little sorrow. It was there that I had learned what it meant to take Jesus with me to work. My attitude toward labor had been changed forever.

I started that job with low expectations, but God had great plans. That work helped form me as a Catholic and as a person. I experienced the satisfaction and the joy of seeing God use me as the channel of his grace for others. I tried to approach that janitorial work with prayer and a Christian attitude, but it was the work of the Holy Spirit that did wonders and even miracles.

Making Christ the Lord of my employment has become central in my life, an integral part of my Christian vocation. Work is an opportunity to serve him and my neighbor. Along with my family and social life, it is a place where God wants to work in me, with me, and through me.

Points to Ponder

Remind them to be ready for any honest work, to speak evil of no one, to avoid quarreling, to be gentle, and to show perfect courtesy toward all men. For we ourselves were once foolish, disobedient, led astray, slaves to various passions and pleasures, passing our days in malice and envy, hated by men and hating one another; but when the goodness and loving kindness of God our Savior appeared, he saved us, not because of deeds done by us in righteousness, but in virtue of his own mercy.

—Titus 3:1–5

Work represents a fundamental dimension of human existence as participation not only in the act of creation but also in that of redemption. Those who put up with the difficult rigors of work in union with Jesus cooperate, in a certain sense, with the Son of God in his work of redemption and show that they are disciples of Christ bearing his cross, every day, in the activity they are called to do. In this perspective, work can be considered a means of sanctification and an enlivening of earthly realities with the Spirit of Christ.[1]

—Pontifical Council for Justice and Peace,
Compendium of the Social Doctrine of the Church

Prayer

Heavenly Father, thank you for the work that lies before me this day. Whether it is for pay or not, I realize that honest work is part of the gift you give me. I desire to do my tasks as unto you. I ask that through my efforts today, your kingdom would be more evident to others.

Discussion Questions and Action Steps

1. Do you know anyone who has fallen away from the Catholic faith? What led him or her away? Consider whether there is something you can do or say to encourage that person to return to the faith. Make a commitment to pray for that person.

2. How can you be a better witness in your workplace, home, or social circle?

3. Reread the quotation from the *Compendium of the Social Doctrine of the Church*. What place does work have in your faith life?

A Punk Rocker Child of God

::: On blessing others :::

Are hospital emergency rooms always crowded on Saturday nights? That was a question on my mind as I waited with my young daughter to see an attending physician. Beverly had injured her eye in a freak accident. It was one of those injuries that was probably not going to be a problem, but seeing a doctor seemed like the most prudent course of action.

While I was trying to calculate how long we might need to wait, a group of six young people burst through the double sliding doors. They appeared to be about eighteen years of age, four men and two women. They were a striking group, and their boisterous entrance caught the attention of everyone in the crowded room.

Each of the six individuals was dressed entirely in black. Two of the young men had insignias on the fronts of their T-shirts, one extolling a "death metal" music group and the other boldly proclaiming, "Satan is great!" Body piercings and tattoos abounded. Thick silver chains adorned their boots and clothing. The only splash of color was in the spiked purple hair of one of the young women.

Two of the youths were holding towels to their heads, covering cuts. The explanation to the attending nurse was that the injuries had occurred when the two had struck each other's heads while "moshing"—a form of violent dance in which the participants jump into each other.

Despite the injuries these youths were far from docile; they were loud, crude, and hyperactive. They did not directly threaten anyone. In fact, they didn't address anyone outside of their own group. Yet their very presence created a sense of dread among the others in the waiting room. Many people left their seats to put distance between themselves and the rowdy group. My young daughter moved closer and snuggled tightly under my protective arm.

I wondered what drug could have created such a state of hyperactivity. And what were these young people capable of? I considered moving to a safer location, yet I hesitated.

The scenario motivated the hospital staff to action. A group of police officers arrived and confronted the group. Voices were raised. Fingers were pointed. Five young people left under police escort, while the most seriously injured youth remained for treatment.

One police officer stayed to watch over the remaining boy, and he ordered the youth to have a seat. The youth slid into a seat directly across from Beverly and me. My daughter looked up at me. There was fear in her hazel-colored eyes. They were pleading for Dad's protection.

I looked at the lad across the aisle. My initial feelings were revulsion as I surveyed the shaved head, the pierced eyebrow, and that shirt that extolled Satan. Yet something was happening in my heart. I glanced again at my daughter, and my love and desire to protect her were overwhelming. When I looked again at the youth, I was surprised to be overwhelmed by a similar sensation. I knew there was a Father who loved this boy and wanted the best for him. Was it the Holy Spirit that was stirring in me?

I felt a mix of pity and fatherly concern for this lad. I also knew that God wanted more for him. Despite his appearance I no longer saw him as threatening. Now he looked alone, isolated, and hurting both physically and spiritually.

A short couple of feet separated us physically. Yet the gulf between us seemed immense. "God, I don't know how to reach this one that you wish to love." This and similar thoughts passed through my mind in a matter of seconds.

Then I was startled as the boy gave a loud and unexpected sneeze. From reflex I reached across the aisle and laid my hand on his knee. The startled youth looked up, and our eyes met for a moment as I said, "God bless you, son." A slight smile crept to the face of the confused youth.

Almost simultaneously the nurse called Beverly to the examination room. As I stood to accompany my daughter, one more smile was exchanged between a black-clad rocker and a conservatively dressed, middle-aged man.

The doctor examined Beverly. She would be fine; there didn't appear to be any significant damage to the eye. We walked back to the waiting room. The young man was gone. I knew that in this life I would probably never see him again.

I reflected on what I had said. "It's just a cultural convention to say, 'God bless you.'" But then I thought, "No, it was more." It had been an opportunity for individuals in two different worlds to touch. Grace had been transferred. I knew that my heart had changed. I would never be able to look at a wildly dressed, tattooed young person in quite the same way. Now when I see a young man like him, a prayer comes to my mind: "God, bless him."

Points to Ponder

Continue steadfastly in prayer.... Conduct yourselves wisely toward outsiders, making the most of the time. Let your speech always be gracious, seasoned with salt, so that you may know how you ought to answer every one.

—Colossians 4:2, 5–6

Let the world know that you have chosen the path of truth, goodness and compassion, honesty and love, pardon and reconciliation where necessary, and openness to all. Yes, the path of generosity, personal discipline and prayer. And when someone asks why you live this way, you will answer: "because of my faith in Jesus Christ." [1]

—John Paul II, homily "Truth, Justice, Peace and Faith to Construct a Better World"

Prayer

I know, Father, that no one is beyond your reach and your mercy. Yet I struggle with how to reach some people with the love of Christ. I ask first that you fill me with love for others, so that I would have the desire to bless them. Then I ask for the wisdom, the timing, and the right words, which only your Holy Spirit can provide.

I pray right now for the young person who is most on my heart. Please bless that youth, and if it be your will, allow me to be a part of that blessing.

Discussion Questions and Action Steps

1. What do you think St. Paul means when he tells us to "conduct ourselves wisely toward strangers" (Colossians 4:5)?

2. What are some of the challenges facing youth in our culture?

3. Choose a young person of your acquaintance. Plan to say an encouraging word to that person, and make a commitment to pray for him or her.

A Pain in the Back

::: On loving my neighbor :::

Author Gary Chapman has written a series of popular books on the five love languages. He tells his readers that there are five predominate ways to show love: words of affirmation, quality time, gift giving, acts of service, and physical touch. He further intimates that individuals usually find a comfort level in one or two of these love expressions.

I am definitely into service love. When you come to the retreat center where I work, I want to carry your bag, make sure that you have everything you need, serve you a meal, and remove the dirty dishes from your table. All eight of us at the retreat center are motivated to serve guests as a part of our expression of service to God. I am definitely working at the right place for my temperament and personality.

However, during the infamous winter snowstorm of February 2010 in Pittsburgh, I injured my back while shoveling the snow that

buried the cars of our guests. I was doing what comes fairly natu-
rally for me—serving my neighbor—but this time there were consequences. I won't bore you with all the details, but the result is that
I now need to avoid heavy lifting if I want to avoid back surgery.

The adjustment has not been easy. I need to check my initial
response. Should I carry that suitcase? Will my back react poorly to
picking up that case of bottled water?

When there has been physical work to do at the retreat center, I've
always tried to pitch in and do my share with my younger coworkers.
Now I must watch as they move furniture or push a wheelbarrow
full of topsoil. It's the same at home: There is just some work that I
can no longer perform.

My wife and coworkers have been very understanding and kind.
In fact, they won't allow me to do anything that might create further injury. If I try to ignore their directions, they reprimand me.
They have no problem with the present situation—my inability to be
involved in physical labor—but I do.

The love language at which I am least adept is "quality time." To
sit and be fully present to another individual does not come natu-
rally to me. I'm often plagued by thoughts of things that I need to
do while I'm trying to reflectively listen to someone. I tend to get
antsy and fidget while trying just to sit still without letting my body
language betray my effort.

I told a friend of my struggle. He told me that he thought that
God wanted me to pray for and with people instead of carting their
belongings up the hill. As soon as he said it, I knew he was right.
The Holy Spirit used that comment to turn on a spiritual light for
me. I knew that God wants to stretch me and get me out of my comfort level and then learn to express love in a different way.

While trying to adjust to my limitations because of the back problem, my wife, whom the Holy Spirit has often used during our more than thirty-five years of marriage to turn on some spiritual lights for me, reminded me of my grandmother's approach. Late in her life, when she was confined to a wheelchair, Libbie and I would go weekly to her home to clean and do the yard work. She would ask, "How long are you planning to stay?" If we said, "Two hours," she would tell us, "Then let's first sit for an hour, have a cup of tea, and visit with each other."

It was always the same. Half of the time we were planning to be there—no matter how long or short and no matter how much work needed to be done—had to be "visiting," and it always had to be the first half. If situations changed and we had to leave early, work could be skipped but never time together.

My grandmother certainly had a servant's heart but one that always functioned within the wider context of relationships. People were always more important than tasks, no matter how important the tasks might seem. Time together always trumped work, even if the floor hadn't been mopped in a week or the grass cut for two. I recall her saying more than once, "When I was a young married woman, I'd dust the windowsills every week. What a waste of time!"

Mary and Martha

I'm not particularly pleased with my bad back, but I think—let me correct that—I know God wants to change and mature me through the consequences of the injury. He is telling me that service is good, but presence to another is of greater value.

Remember Martha, the sister of Lazarus and Mary? Service love apparently was her love language as well. In her I find a kindred spirit. Meanwhile, her sister Mary was like my grandmother. She found delight in "visiting" with the Lord.

Jesus gave the active sister a mild rebuke: "Martha, Martha, you are anxious and worried about many things. There is need of only one thing. Mary has chosen the better part, and it will not be taken away from her" (Luke 10:41–42, *NAB*). The "better part!"

Jesus wasn't condemning Martha for her work. I'm sure there was great benefit from it—a comfortable environment, a good meal, and so on. I'm sure Jesus appreciated it. In fact, some biblical scholars, reflecting on Jesus' words to Martha, point out that the repetition of Martha's name was a sign of affection. Yet Martha's work for her divine guest will always be in second place and must be at the service of the better part, the relationship to the other.

I'm still struggling, but I know that, since God is calling me to get better in this area, he will also continue to give me grace to improve. He will continue to use my friends, coworkers, and wife to nudge me in the right direction.

My grandmother, on the other hand, died many years ago, so she can no longer audibly remind me that cleaning the windowsills can be a waste of time. She now is probably sitting at the same feet at which Mary sat in that home in Bethany of Judea. I'm sure she is listening and, when appropriate, asking the Lord to help this slow learner in western Pennsylvania. Thanks, Grandma!

Points to Ponder

> To draw near to listen is better than to offer the sacrifice of fools.
>
> —Ecclesiastes 5:1

> I always follow this principle: I welcome everyone as a person sent to me and entrusted to me by Christ.[1]
>
> —Blessed Pope John Paul II, *Rise, Let Us Be on Our Way*

A smile is the beginning of love. [2]

—Mother Teresa

Prayer

"He who has ears, let him hear" (Matthew 13:9). Eternal Word of the Father, I tend to be deaf to your words and to those of others. I'm so busy and concerned with my own agenda that I don't stop to listen. I'm prone to miss "the better part." Yet I know that to love you and others well, I must be fully present and engaged with the speaker.

Forgive me for the idolatry of being so concerned with the things of this world that I fail to listen to you. Forgive me for failing to uphold the dignity of each person when I value activity more than the individual. Grant me ears that hear. Grant me a heart that opens to you and to my neighbor. May it be so. Amen.

Discussion Questions and Action Steps

1. What is your "love language"? How do you demonstrate it?
2. What is the "love language" with which you are least comfortable? How can you grow in your use of it?
3. Explore the meaning of active and reflective listening. How well do you listen to God? To others?

A Hero and an Angel

::: On the works of mercy :::

As director of the Catholic Cemetery Association in Tucson, I regularly saw tragedy. Drive-by shootings, suicides, and children dying of cancer are events with which I never got comfortable. We did what we could to assist people in their sorrow. We encouraged and provided respectful burial for all: the rich and the poor, the stillborn infant and the elderly individual with no family.

In particular, we made the decision to bury all infants for free. It was our way of saying that miscarriages and stillborns had held the breath of God. They, as all human life, are deserving of respectful burial. We buried about seventy infants a year.

There is one such burial that I will never forget. I was in my office when I received a call on our radio system that there was no priest or deacon to conduct the committal for an infant. I grabbed my committal book and headed for the grave. There I found four people gathered. One was the driver from the funeral home. Two were my employees. The other was a young woman who sobbed quietly as she looked down at a small white casket that sat on two boards over a small grave.

In a quick conversation with the funeral home representative, I learned that the young woman was nineteen years old and had conceived her child out of wedlock. Her family had disowned her because of her situation. The young man who had fathered the child wanted no part of parenting; when the young woman stuck with her commitment to carry the child, he too deserted her.

I have no idea how this girl survived alone. Where did she work? Who encouraged her in her decision not to abort? Who comforted her in her sorrow? I am sure that the journey was not easy. Nonetheless she carried her child to almost full term, only to deliver the infant stillborn.

The young woman had no car; she had taken a bus to the cemetery. I asked if we were to wait for anyone else. She softly replied that there would be no others. Two other cemetery employees joined us as we began the committal prayers. These men who daily dealt with death were deeply moved as we shared the loss with this woman.

Someone took the hand of the grieving mother. We all silently followed the gesture by joining hands with one another as I began the prayers. With a trembling hand the mother took the container of holy water that I offered to her, giving a final blessing to the casket containing the body of her child. I told her that we would all continue to pray for her.

As I looked up at the end of our prayer, I noticed another young woman, who must have been visiting a nearby grave. She had moved closer to our group and apparently had joined in our prayer. Placing her hand on the girl's shoulder, she explained that her infant son had been buried in a nearby grave. Her arm encircled the nineteen-year-old girl and drew her close. "Please, let me drive you home. I know how you feel right now."

The nineteen-year-old allowed her head to drop to the shoulder of the other woman, as she continued to sob. Together they paid their last respects at the grave and walked slowly to a car. To some it may have looked as if two losers were leaving the cemetery. However, we who had shared those moments knew that a real hero and an angel had been in our midst.

Some who are called heroes earn that title through a one-time decision; every day for nine months this woman made the heroic decision to say yes to life. I have never met anyone more heroic. I only wish I had had the grace to tell her so that day.

Yet this nineteen-year-old was never truly alone. God was with her every step of the way. I hope that she felt his comfort often. I know she must have sensed his strength with her. I witnessed at least one of his mercies when on that day at the cemetery, he sent a woman, an angel, to hold this child of God, share her tears, and provide a strong shoulder for support.

The example of these two women speaks to us. We too are to live heroic virtue as articulated in the Beatitudes and the works of mercy[1] (see below). We are not alone in our efforts, because Jesus, the all-virtuous, gives his strength to us and through us to others.

Points to Ponder

The Beatitudes

Blessed are the poor in spirit, for theirs is the kingdom of heaven.
Blessed are those who mourn, for they shall be comforted.
Blessed are the meek, for they shall inherit the earth.
Blessed are those who hunger and thirst for righteousness, for they shall be satisfied.
Blessed are the merciful, for they shall obtain mercy.

Blessed are the pure in heart, for they shall see God.

Blessed are the peacemakers, for they shall be called sons of
God.

Blessed are those who are persecuted for righteousness'
sake, for theirs is the kingdom of heaven.

Blessed are you when men revile you and persecute you and
utter all kinds of evil against you falsely on my account.
Rejoice and be glad, for your reward is great in heaven, for
so men persecuted the prophets who were before you.

—Matthew 5:3–12

The corporal works of mercy:
- feed the hungry;
- give drink to the thirsty;
- clothe the naked;
- shelter the homeless;
- visit the sick;
- visit the imprisoned;
- bury the dead.

The spiritual works of mercy:
- instruct the ignorant;
- counsel the doubtful;
- admonish sinners;
- bear wrongs patiently;
- forgive offenses willingly;
- comfort the afflicted;
- pray for the living and the dead.

Prayer

Dear Lord, our culture is in urgent need of heroes and angels. From
major issues, such as abortion, assisted suicide, and war, and from

issues that seem smaller but have effects often more immediate, such as lonely people, angry drivers, and children on drugs, we are a seriously wounded generation that finds itself in peril. Nothing less than men and women empowered by you, emboldened by the Holy Spirit, and reliant upon the Father will meet our need.

Lord, send us heroes and angels. And let me, weak and frightened as I am, be among their number.

Discussion Questions and Action Steps

1. Which of the Beatitudes do you find most striking? Why?
2. What can you do to encourage a culture of life in our society?
3. You can find *Evangelium Vitae* by Blessed Pope John Paul II on the Internet. Read portions of the encyclical. (I recommend section 22.) In your own words summarize what you have read.

Taking the Plunge

::: On imitating Christ, who gave his life for us sinners :::

Almost every family has at least one individual who can only be classified as "a character." In my extended family that person was my great-uncle Cornelius.

Nell, as everyone called him, was the third of ten children. Having served in World War I, he had a rough exterior, and his speech was often "colorful." But he possessed a heart of gold. He would help anyone who needed his assistance.

An unforgettable event occurred when Nell was a young man. After a day's work he was walking home, when he saw a man jump from a bridge into the water below in an attempt to commit suicide. Nell immediately jumped in the water and pulled the man to safety. In the process he lost his new hat.

When Nell got home, family members asked him, "Where's your new hat?" Nell's simple response was "Lost it." The full story only became known the next day, when the family read in the newspaper that Cornelius had saved a man from drowning.

Reflection of a Greater One

Some people would say that Nell was foolish to endanger his own life to save someone who was committing suicide. In fact, the man who had jumped from the bridge later successfully killed himself. Yet Nell's plunge into the river reflected the actions of his Savior.

Our human race tried to commit suicide in the Garden of Eden. God had told our first parents, "You may freely eat of every tree of the garden; but of the tree of the knowledge of good and evil you shall not eat, for in the day that you eat of it you shall die" (Genesis 2:16–17). Nevertheless, Adam and Eve plucked the forbidden fruit and ate it. They were committing suicide. Thankfully, God was not only all-just but also all-merciful. So the Second Person of the Holy Trinity took a plunge for us. He became man to save us from certain and eternal death.

Nell lost his new hat because he valued the life of that man more than some material item. Christ set aside something of infinitely greater value when he became a man. St. Paul writes, "Christ Jesus, ...though he was in the form of God, did not count equality with God a thing to be grasped, but emptied himself, taking the form of a servant" (Philippians 2:5–7).

Jesus embraced a most ignominious death on the cross to save us. What is more, he knew that some of those for whom he died would later commit "suicide" anyway. In his agony in the Garden of Gethsemane, surely part of Christ's suffering was the realization that some people would reject the salvation he offered through his death. It is then even more amazing that Christ chose to die for us anyway.

The practice of charity and good works was a regular part of Nell's life. He also never made a "big deal" about the good that he did. You and I are likewise called to good works, both of the physical and spiritual variety. We are to love not only our friends but even our enemies (see Matthew 5:44). We are to give even when our good deeds might be rejected or misunderstood (Luke 6:30–35). Putting aside fear, we must lay down our lives for others in imitation of Christ (John 15:12–13). God gives us the grace to do what we are tempted to see as impossible.

God gives us a heavenly intercessor who was also a tremendous help to my great-uncle. Nell had a devotion to the Blessed Mother and always carried his rosary. Jesus gave his mother to us before he took his final breath on the cross (see John 19:26–27). We can turn to her in our struggles.

Mary took a great risk when she said yes to the angel who conveyed the message that she would be the mother of the Savior. Her heart would be pierced often as she shared in her son's mission. She identifies too with us in our struggles. Our mom in heaven will pray for us and stand with us as we seek the perfection of Christ in our lives.

Points to Ponder
(Note: This Scripture passage speaks of alms, but the principle is true for any good work.)

> Thus, when you give alms, sound no trumpet before you, as the hypocrites do in the synagogues and in the streets, that they may be praised by men. Truly, I say to you, they have their reward. But when you give alms, do not let your left hand know what your right hand is doing, so that your alms may be in secret; and your Father who sees in secret will reward you.
>
> —Matthew 6:2–4

The Word became flesh *to be our model of holiness*.... Jesus is the model for the Beatitudes and the norm of the new law: "Love one another as I have loved you" [John 15:12]. This love implies an effective offering of oneself, after his example.

—*Catechism of the Catholic Church*, #459

Prayer

The *Memorare*

Remember, O most gracious Virgin Mary,

that never was it known

that anyone who fled to your protection, implored your help, or

 sought your intercession

was left unaided.

Inspired by this confidence, I fly unto you,

O Virgin of virgins, my mother;

to you do I come, before you I stand, sinful and sorrowful.

O Mother of the Word Incarnate,

despise not my petitions,

but in your mercy hear and answer me. Amen.

Discussion Questions and Action Steps

1. What was the cost of our salvation?
2. What consequences do our sins have?
3. Read 2 Timothy 2. How can you share in Christ's redemptive work?

Wrestling With God
::: On conversion :::

Do you remember the story of Jacob (beginning at Genesis 25:19)? One of the patriarchs, he was the son of Isaac and the grandson of Abraham. God eventually changed his name to Israel. A nation bearing that name grew from his offspring.

However, Jacob did not have a very auspicious beginning to his life. In fact, he was far from a paragon of virtue—an unlikely character from whom to establish a nation.

In the culture of Jacob's time, the oldest son would inherit the wealth, governance, and prestige of his father. Jacob missed that privilege by a matter of minutes. He was one of a set of twins, and he was born second. In fact, Scripture reports that Jacob was born clutching the heel of his brother, Esau. Jacob would spend the early part of his life trying to catch up to Esau but only able to grasp his heel.

Esau was a rugged individualist—a man's man, if you will—who found favor with his father because of his hunting skills and physical strength. Apparently Jacob was more of a mommy's boy. Perhaps that is why he was only number two in his father's eye.

Jacob, at his mother's urging, aspired to greatness. He wanted to inherit the leadership of the family after the death of his father. Jacob used manipulation, trickery, and deceit to acquire what he desired.

For example, Jacob got Esau to sell his birthright to him in exchange for food. Not a very brotherly approach. And when the almost blind Isaac was dying, Jacob tricked him into giving him the blessing that was normally reserved for the eldest son and was a means of passing on authority. As I mentioned, Jacob was not a paragon of virtue! His mother arranged for him to leave town to escape the wrath of his brother.

In exile Jacob met the woman he wanted to marry, the beautiful Rachel. Rachel's father, Laban, was not about to let Jacob marry his daughter unless he got something in return. So Jacob agreed to work for seven years to win her hand.

At the appointed time the deceiver was deceived: Laban substituted his older daughter, Leah, in place of Rachel. Jacob then needed to work an additional seven years for the opportunity to marry Rachel.

This Old Testament version of a soap opera had still more episodes. Jacob managed to anger his father-in-law by some creative shepherding and then had to flee as he had fled from Esau. He headed back to the place of his birth.

Jacob was in a fearful situation. Behind him was a none too happy father-in-law, and in front of him was the aggrieved Esau. This was the pivotal moment in Jacob's life. In this conundrum he had a new openness to God. Do we not often turn to God with fervor only when we are in a difficult situation?

Genesis 32 tells the story. "Jacob said, 'O God of my father Abraham and God of my father Isaac.... Deliver me, I beg you, from the hand of my brother, from the hand of Esau, for I fear him, lest he come and slay us all'" (verses 9, 11).

God heard this prayer and sent his representative to Jacob. The Scripture records that Jacob wrestled with God's representative.[1] It was quite a battle, and Jacob didn't give up until he received God's blessing. God also opened Esau's heart to graciously receive his younger brother.

This story certainly shows us that God hears our prayers, and it encourages us to persevere in beseeching God.[2] Yet I think the most important part of the story occurred after God agreed to bless Jacob. The Scripture records that God's messenger "touched the hollow of his thigh; and Jacob's thigh was put out of joint as he wrestled with him" (Genesis 32:25). One result of the encounter was that Jacob walked with a limp (see Gen 32:31). That limp was a reminder that Jacob had met God and been changed—converted—by the encounter.

Jacob's life was dramatically transformed. He developed a more personal relationship with God by wrestling with him. Before this event Jacob called upon the God of "Abraham and Isaac." After the wrestling match Jacob could refer to God as "the God who answered me in the day of my distress and has been with me wherever I had gone" (Genesis 35:3). He knew him then as the God of Jacob.

It must be the same with us. God wants to touch us and change us in a way that will affect our lives. So we need not be afraid to wrestle with God! Take your struggles to him, and come to know the God of_____. (This is where you can fill in your name!)

Points to Ponder

In many of the psalms the author struggles with God; he wants to know where God is in the midst of his difficulties. This is not rebellion but rather a heartfelt desire to know God's will and receive his guidance and blessing. Psalm 13 is one example. Note the change in the author's outlook between the questions that begin the psalm and the resolution at the end.

> How long, O LORD? Will you forget me forever?
>   How long will you hide your face from me?
> How long must I bear pain in my soul,
>   and have sorrow in my heart all the day?
> How long shall my enemy be exalted over me?
>
> Consider and answer me, O LORD my God;
>   lighten my eyes, lest I sleep the sleep of death;
> lest my enemy say, "I have prevailed over him";
>   lest my foes rejoice because I am shaken.
>
> But I have trusted in your merciful love;
>   my heart shall rejoice in your salvation.
> I will sing to the LORD,
>   because he has dealt bountifully with me.

God tirelessly calls each person to this mysterious encounter with Himself.

—Catechism of the Catholic Church, #2591

Prayer

Pray Psalm 13 above, but personalize it, telling your heavenly Father where you are struggling right now. Ask him for guidance and blessing. Be open to his touch, and trust in his love.

Discussion Questions and Action Steps

1. When we wrestle with God, the key to victory is losing the competition! God has the answer to our problems and wants to lead us in ways of truth. The first step is to bring our problems and concerns to him. Then as he reveals himself, we yield. How can you be better prepared to yield to God in any and all encounters with him?

2. When have you wrestled with God over a challenge in your life? What was the problem you faced, and how was it resolved? Can you see God's action in the resolution? How so?

3. Jacob's troubles sprang from damaged family relationships (problems with his brother and father-in-law). What relationship in your life is in most need of healing? What practical steps can you take to improve that relationship?

A Fellow Human Being
::: On the dignity of every person :::

In September of 1994 my youngest brother was well established, well respected, and moving up the corporate ladder in the largest bank in Pittsburgh. He was also a very likable young man. In any and every conversation, he was most concerned about what the other person had to say rather than what was on his mind. He was kind and funny.

Kevin was married to a wonderful woman and had two small children. He was wholeheartedly committed to his family. That is what prompted him to fly home early from a business trip in Chicago.

He was scheduled to fly back to Pittsburgh the next day. However, when his meeting finished sooner than expected, he headed to the airport in hopes of catching a flight. He called his wife to tell her that, if a seat was available, he'd see her later that evening.

He did get a seat on a flight, but he never made it home. USAir flight 427 crashed as it was approaching the Pittsburgh International Airport. All 132 people on board perished.

The line of mourners and well-wishers at the funeral home seemed unending. We, his family, knew that he was a wonderful man, but it was almost overwhelming to see how many other people he had touched in his brief life. They included people he knew from grade school, high school, and college, neighbors, coworkers, business associates, and even people who had only secondhand knowledge of him. Most had a story that they wanted to share on how he had affected their life.

There was one visitor who summarized my brother's life and whose testimony touched us more than any other. He was the barber who had a shop on the first floor of the skyscraper where my brother worked. Because his shop was so conveniently located, he cut the hair of many, if not most, of the men in that building.

In twenty years the barber had never closed his shop early on a regular business day; he had closed early this day so he could attend Kevin's wake. As he shook my hand, he told me how highly he respected my brother and that he even considered him a friend. He said, "To most people I'm just a barber; to your brother I was a fellow human being."

The Dignity of the Person

The Church has always upheld the dignity of each and every person. After all, Jesus died for all men, even for those who reject him. If Jesus found each of us worthy of his shed blood, how could we act otherwise?

In truth, there are only two types of people in this world. Some are in the family of God through baptism and are therefore our brothers and sisters. All others are potential brothers and sisters, whom Christ also wants to draw into his great family.

Like any family we are a diverse group. Some live exemplary lives; others live only for themselves. Some are trying to walk as faithful as possible to Christ's teaching; others are prodigals. Some we will see in heaven, while others will, in the end, choose hell. Yet the truth remains: Everyone we meet is either a brother or sister or a potential brother or sister. There are no other categories.

Family life demands love for all members. Think of the love of our heavenly Father, whose arms are open to receive his children, as Jesus revealed in the story of the Prodigal Son (see Luke 15:11–32). Think of Jesus, our elder brother, the firstborn in the faith, whose arms are also outstretched on the cross, from which drips the blood that cleanses and saves.

Now think of me; think of you. We must open our arms as well, in imitation of our Father and Brother. Every—every—person has value and deserves to be treated with dignity. Family life demands it.

Points to Ponder

[God] did not spare his own Son but gave him up for us all.

—Romans 8:32

In a special way, believers in Christ must defend and promote this right [the sacred value of human life from conception until natural death], aware as they are of the wonderful truth recalled by the Second Vatican Council: "By his incarnation the Son of God has united himself in some fashion with *every* human being" [*Gaudium et Spes*, 22]. This saving event reveals to humanity not only the boundless love of God who "so loved the world that he gave his only Son" (John 3.16), but also the incomparable value of *every* human person. [1]

—Blessed Pope John Paul II, *Evangelium Vitae*

Prayer

> O Virgin Mother,
> guide and sustain us
> so that we might always live
> as true sons and daughters
> of the Church of your Son.
> Enable us to do our part
> in helping to establish on earth
> the civilization of truth and love,
> as God wills it,
> for his glory.
> Amen. [2]

—Blessed Pope John Paul II, *Christifideles Laici*

Discussion Questions and Action Steps

1. Read paragraph 1700 of the *Catechism of the Catholic Church* on the dignity of the human person. Summarize in your own words what you have read.

2. How well is the dignity of every person upheld in society?

3. What practical actions can you take to witness to the dignity of each and every person?

The Best Wine

::: On how God can bless others through us :::

I try to live my faith, seek God's will, and obey the nudgings of the Holy Spirit. Nonetheless, I have quite a long list of shortcomings, failures, and sins that still plague me. So it always leaves me in awe when God chooses to work through me to bless someone. In my opinion it is always a miracle.

I'm reminded of the story of the wedding feast of Cana. Jesus took some common earthen vessels, had the servants fill them with water, and then changed that water into wine. That wine was so choice that the head steward remarked, "Everyone serves good wine first, and then when people have drunk freely, an inferior one; but you have kept the good wine until now" (John 2:10, *NAB*).

Surely you and I are only common vessels filled with holy water. It is good to be so constructed and to be so filled that we can bring refreshment to others. As baptized Christians we are water for a parched world, salt for a culture that needs the flavor of God's work (see Mark 9:50), and a beacon that sheds light in the darkness

(Matthew 5:14–16). To that we can say an alleluia!

However, God wants to do more through us. Let me give you an example.

My wife and I have had a few people live in our home while trying to help them through times of difficulty. One young woman, I'll call her Marie, lived with us for a time and then moved out to be on her own. She continued to visit us regularly. In fact, we viewed her as another one of our daughters. Then, one day my wife told me that Marie was again struggling.

While praying for Marie on my drive home, it struck me that perhaps a few carnations would cheer her. So I stopped at the florist. As I was ordering the carnations, I noticed that a large floral arrangement featuring roses was on sale. On an impulse I told the clerk, "Forget the carnations; I'll take those flowers with the roses instead."

Once back in the car, I felt a little awkward. Roses are for your sweetheart more than for your daughter. But the purchase had been made; it would have to do.

When I arrived at Marie's apartment, she wasn't home. A bit sheepishly, I left the flowers in front of her door, with a note that Libbie and I were praying for her.

Later that evening we received a phone call from Marie. Excitedly she told us that she had just finished a novena to St. Thérèse of Lisieux—the saint who promised to shower roses from heaven upon those who sought her intercession. That floral arrangement with all the roses was a confirmation to Marie that the saint had indeed heard the prayers she had offered over that nine-day novena. The chain of blessing was from God through St. Thérèse and then through me to Marie.

Availability and Expectation

God can do what he wants, in whatever way he wants. After all, he is, well, God. However, he often chooses to use those who make themselves available to him.

The Little Flower, St. Thérèse of Lisieux, made herself available to God during her earthly life and continues to do so from the heavenly realm. God worked through her to bless people and still does so today. The key is that she was, and is, available to God. We should be the same.

St. Thérèse and God get 99.99 percent of the credit for the blessing that Marie received. However, I was a part of the deal. I was praying for Marie, asking God to bless her. My heart was set on finding a way to help the young woman. I walked into the florist and put the money down on the counter to pay for the flowers that the Holy Spirit and St. Thérèse pointed out to me—even though at the moment I would have called it an impulse and not the Spirit's work.

Availability to God is an important component of the miracles that he wishes to work through his children and for his children. Every morning in my prayers, I ask God to work through me that day to bless someone. I'm only a stone pot of water, but Jesus has his hands extended over me in prayer. I can be the choice wine for someone or some ones during the upcoming day.

When I say my final prayers in the evening, I examine myself. Was I available to God working through me that day? How so? I then give thanks or repent as may be necessary.

In addition to availability, expectation is helpful. During each day, as we go through our various duties, we can be on the lookout for where, when, and how God might want to work in and through us. He will show us.

Points to Ponder

How admirable the plan, the universal law laid down by Providence, that it is through men, that men are to find out the way to salvation. Jesus Christ alone has shed the Blood that redeems the world. Alone, too, he might have put its power to work, and acted upon souls directly, as he does in the Holy Eucharist. But he wanted to have others cooperate in the distribution of his graces. Why? No doubt his divine Majesty demanded that it be so, but his loving affection for men urged him no less. And if it is seemly for the most exalted king to govern, more often than not, through ministers, what condescension it is for God to deign to give poor creatures a share in his work and in his glory![1]

—Dom Jean-Baptiste Chautard, *The Soul of the Apostolate*

In a great house there are not only vessels of gold and silver but also of wood and earthenware, and some for noble use, some for ignoble. If any one purifies himself from what is ignoble, then he will be a vessel for noble use, consecrated and useful to the master of the house, ready for any good work.

—2 Timothy 2:20–21

Prayer

Lord, use me today to bless someone, and let it be done for your glory and for the love of my neighbor.

Discussion Questions and Action Steps

1. Recall an incident in which you experienced God's blessing through the action of someone else.

2. Have you ever experienced being God's hands of blessing to another person? Explain.

3. Recall the life of one of the saints. How did that saint yield to God's work of blessing others? Ask that saint to intercede for you, especially that you would be a willing vessel for "noble use."

T-shirt Theology
::: On the dignity of man in the sight of God :::

As I mentioned previously, I've always enjoyed playing basketball. I often tell people that I was the team's twenty-point man. I wait for the inevitable nod of amazement before finishing my sentence, "Yes, I only got into the game if our team was winning or losing by twenty points." In truth, I was the perennial benchwarmer.

Knowing my dedication to the game, despite my lack of proficiency, my wife once bought me a T-shirt with a picture of a basketball and the words "Basketball is life. The rest is just details." I still enjoy basketball, but I'm most grateful that it is not "life." If it was I would have no chance to be a winner!

Our culture presents to us a variety of definitions of the essence of life: athletic ability, youth, money, popularity, good looks, power, sensuality, money, and so on. If any of these are the definition of life, I think that most of us have little hope of success. We are destined to be perennial benchwarmers.

Thanks be to God that he has another definition of life—one that positions us to successfully compete in the game. We can aspire to the greatest heights—how far is heaven above earth?—when we know who we are and what God has done for each of us. The *Catechism of the Catholic Church*, in the very first article of the very first section of the text, gives us the true essence of the life of man: "God, infinitely perfect and blessed in himself, in a plan of sheer goodness freely created man to make him share in his own blessed life" (*CCC*, #1). This first statement of the *Catechism*, I believe, should be primary in all our thinking. In fact, it's the basis for everything else in our lives.

We have been loved into being by the infinitely perfect God. It was his sheer goodness that brought you and me to life. We are not mistakes or afterthoughts. He intends that we share in the blessedness that he enjoys for all eternity. This gives us perspective on the entirety of our lives.

The dignity we have as beings created in God's image—fashioned, we are told, as the crown of creation—is a breathtaking reality. Here is what the psalmist writes:

> What are humans that you are mindful of them,
>   mere mortals that you care for them?
> Yet you have made them little less than a god,
>   crowned them with glory and honor.
> You have given them rule over the works of your hands,
>   put all things at their feet.
>   —Psalm 8:5–7, *NAB*

Blood Has Been Shed for Us

Yet God has honored you and me even more. God became man. The Second Person of the Trinity took on flesh, and then he did the unthinkable: He died an ignominious death for us. The same Love that created us shed his blood for us. As St. Paul writes so eloquently, "Christ Jesus, ... though he was in the form of God, did not count equality with God a thing to be grasped, but emptied himself, taking the form of a servant, being born in the likeness of men. And being found in human form he humbled himself and became obedient unto death, even death on a cross" (Philippians 2:5b–8).

How often have we heard those words? It's tempting to read them quickly as something we already know. Yet what God did for us is creation shaking (see Matthew 27:51). It leaves even angels in awe (Revelation 5:6–14). We need to regularly ruminate on Paul's words. They reveal a truth that should color how we view ourselves and everyone else.

Our dignity rests on the fact that Love created us and the shed blood of Love redeemed us. Yet even this was not enough for God. He has done even more for us.

Jesus identified so closely with us that he now calls us his brothers and sisters, and truly we are. Our identification with him makes us children of God. The beloved disciple of Jesus writes to us, "Beloved, we are God's children now" (1 John 3:2; see also Romans 8:16).

It is through baptism that we become children of God. We enter the waters estranged from him because of sin and rise as family members with Jesus as brother, with the Father in heaven as our own, and with the Holy Spirit tying us all together.

I'm most thankful that my parents gave me the name *Regis* at my baptism. From the Latin my name can be translated "son of the king." The dignity I have because I was created and redeemed by Love was deepened when I went through the waters of the sacrament. In truth I became Regis, a son of the King. You who read this, if you have been baptized, are also "regis." We are all sons and daughters of the King of Creation.

Baptism creates an unbreakable relationship. The *Catechism* states that we are indelibly marked as belonging to God (see *CCC*, #1272–1274). We may be prodigal and wander, but our heavenly Father has the same attitude as the father in the parable of the Prodigal Son. He still sees us as his children. His arms are always open wide to receive us. If the circumstances of life are beating us down, we can, and we should, stop, look up, and state the truth: "I am not just any Tom, Dick, Harry, Mary, Jane, or Ann. I am a son (daughter) of the King! I have dignity. I am loved."

We don't need to buy into the lies that the world, our weak flesh, and the devil whisper to us. No, we can look beyond the transitory and affirm from where—from whom—we have come.

Practical Implications

No matter what my present circumstances, I know I was created and redeemed by God, who loves me. What is more, I am a child of God. That is the solid ground of truth from which I move forward. If I need to repent, I repent as a child of God. If I'm tempted, I can muster my defenses because Jesus shed his blood for me. If I need to fight the good fight of faith (see 1 Timothy 1:18), I can do so because God created me to share life with him. God is with me and for me, and that makes a world of difference for me.

Knowing who we are will help us make right decisions, overcome obstacles, and generally live the life to which God calls us. Established on firm footing, we can move forward.

Actually, I think someone should make a T-shirt that really proclaims the truth. It should have a picture of Our Lord blessing a person. Then the words superimposed on the picture could be "Life is in God. The rest is just details." I'd be proud to wear that one.

Points to Ponder

Before I formed you in the womb I knew you,
and before you were born I consecrated you.

—Jeremiah 1:5

By his incarnation Christ became poor to enrich us with his
poverty, and he gave us redemption, which is the fruit above
all of the blood he shed on the Cross.[1]

—Blessed Pope John Paul II, Homily at
World Youth Day 1999

Prayer

At times, Lord, I am confused. I feel downtrodden, even defeated.
At times it is hard to see you, and I feel overwhelmed by the circumstances that surround me. Help me at those moments to call to
mind the person I am in you. I have been created in your image; I
have been redeemed by your blood; you are my brother, and we
share the same Father. What dignity I possess! What dignity you
have given to all men and women!

Let that knowledge be my source of perspective and esteem. Let
me view others as worthy of respect because of that same dignity.
With the psalmist I pray,

I praise you, so wonderfully you made me;
wonderful are your works! (Psalm 139:14, *NAB*)
Thank you, Lord!

Discussion Questions and Action Steps

1. Some people proclaim their beliefs with words on a T-shirt or a
   bumper sticker. Recall one that you have seen recently. Is it consistent with teachings of the Catholic Church? Why or why not?

2. If you were designing a T-shirt proclaiming your belief, what would you imprint on it? Why?

3. Knowing who we are in Christ can help us overcome timidity and fear. Is there an attitude in your life keeping you from living with confidence in God?

Conclusion
::: On moving forward :::

When I was asked to write this book, I was more than delighted. As I mentioned in the introduction, God has often taught me through events. It has been a great blessing to recall some of those stories, dig through my old journals, and discuss with my wife and my family the "remember whens" of our lives.

As I come to the conclusion of this edition, I find myself most thankful for the good work that God has achieved in me, through me, and yes, often despite me. I am also convinced that I am still very much a work in progress. I don't know how many more years or days God will keep me in this world, but I know he has plans for that remaining time period. The journey goes on, and there are events yet to come and stories yet to be written. Reflecting on where I have been nudges me to consider where I need to go—to repent and be more deeply converted, to yield more to God, and to seek him in all aspects of my life.

If my stories have in some way encouraged you, perhaps you would want to share some of your stories with me. I'd be delighted to hear them, both for my edification and for the glory of God. Perhaps my next book could be your tales rather than mine. You can e-mail me at RegisJFlaherty@gmail.com.

Notes

Introduction

1. Pontifical Biblical Commission, *The Interpretation of the Bible in the Church*, March 18, 1994, I.B.2, emphasis added. Available at http://www.ewtn.com.

Chapter 1: Can You Give Me a Witness?

1. Josemaría Escrivá, "Passionately Loving the World," chap. 8, no. 115, in *Conversations with Monsignor Escrivá de Balaguer*, available at www.escrivaworks.org.

2. Pope Paul VI, *Evangelii Nuntiandi*, Apostolic Exhortation, no. 41, December 8, 1975, www.vatican.va, quoting his Address to the Members of the Consilium de Laicis, October 2, 1974.

Chapter 2: Embracing Obedience

1. Vatican Council II, *Dogmatic Constitution on the Church*, no. 37, www.vatican.va.

Chapter 3: "Who's the Boss Here?"

1. Information on a home enthronement of the Sacred Heart is available at several websites.

2. Pope Pius XI, *Quas Primas*, Encyclical on the Feast of Christ the King, no. 26, December 11, 1925, www.vatican.va.

3. This prayer is taken from an enthronement ceremony in Appendix II of Scott Hahn and Regis J. Flaherty, eds., *Catholic for a Reason IV: Scripture and the Mystery of Marriage and Family Life* (Steubenville, Ohio: Emmaus Road, 2007), pp. 187–194.

Chapter 4: Flecte Genu

1. Thomas Aquinas, *Summa Theologica*, II-II, ques. 84, art. 2, reply objs. 1, 2, and 3, www.newadvent.org.

Chapter 5: An Answer in the Mail

1. A novena consists of nine days of prayer for a specific intention. It harkens back to the nine days of prayer between Christ's ascension and Pentecost. During this period the disciples were gathered together in the Upper Room, prayerfully awaiting the move of the Holy Spirit.

2. There are times when a civil divorce may be necessary, such as for protection in an abusive situation. But for validly married couples, the sacrament remains in force until one partner dies. An annulment is not a divorce. It is a declaration by a Church court that a true marriage never existed.

3. Pope John Paul II, Homily "True Human Love Reflects the Divine," September 25, 1993, no. 4, www.catholic-forum.com.

Chapter 6: A Delayed Response

1. "Following recognition by the Holy See, the United States Conference of Catholic Bishops has decreed that the age for conferring the sacrament of confirmation in the Latin Rite dioceses of the United States will be between 'the age of discretion and about sixteen years of age.' ...The decree becomes effective July 1, 2002" (www.usccb.org).

2. I followed up by receiving the sacrament of reconciliation before the end of the retreat.

3. One can enter a valid marriage more than once but only if one's first spouse has died.

Chapter 7: What I Have I Give to You?

1. Pope John Paul II, Message on the Occasion of the Thirteenth World Youth Day, November 30, 1997, no. 4, www.vatican.va.

Chapter 8: A Healthy Shot in the Arm

1. Blasphemy and cursing are sins against the second command-ment. To blaspheme is to speak of God or use his name in an irreverent way; cursing is an appeal that evil fall upon someone or on a situation. Many people blaspheme and curse without a formed intent to be irreverent or to call down evil. Nonetheless, these are serious sins because they are direct offenses against God and, in the case of cursing, other people.

   Certainly all Catholics should avoid these sins. Also, if someone close to you blasphemes or curses, it's appropriate to call the serious nature of these sins to his or her attention. These sins should offend us because they are aimed at Our Lord, someone whom we love deeply and who loves us infinitely.

   Vulgarities are failures of refinement. While they are offensive, they are not materially as serious as curses and blasphemies. They are sinful when they disparage that which is intended to be holy. For many people the use of vulgarity is a habit that reflects a lack—perhaps unintended—of reverence for creation and therefore for the Creator.

Chapter 9: Isn't That Nice?

1. Elisabeth Elliot, quoting Jim Elliot; see *Shadow of the Almighty: The Life and Testament of Jim Elliot* (New York: Hendrickson, 2008), p. 43.

2. Pope Benedict XV, *Humani Generis Redemptionem*, Encyclical Letter on Preaching the Word of God, no. 19, June 15, 1917, www.vatican.va.

Chapter 12: Where Is Your Heart?

1. Thomas à Kempis, *The Imitation of Christ*, book 2, chap. 7 (Brooklyn: Confraternity of the Precious Blood, 1954), p. 125.

Chapter 13: Make a Memorial and Visit It Often

1. Second Council of Nicaea, *Nicene and Post-Nicene Fathers*, second series, vol. 14 (Peabody, Mass.: Hendrickson, 1994), p. 541, also available at www.ccel.org.

Chapter 14: Alive in the Sky

1. See Augustine, *Confessions*, bk. 1, chap. 1.

2. Pope Paul VI, Apostolic Letter *Solemni Hac Liturgia*, "The Credo of the People of God," no. 28, June 30, 1968, www.vatican.va.

3. I've written a book that deals extensively with this topic. See *Last Things First* (Huntington, Ind.: Our Sunday Visitor, 2005).

Chapter 15: Lenten Sacrifices

1. Josemaría Escrivá, "The Richness of Ordinary Life," no. 7 in *Friends of God: Homilies by Josemaría Escrivá* (Princeton, N.J.: Scepter, 1981), p. 8. Available at www.escrivaworks.org.

Chapter 16: Fluffy Towels

1. Pope Benedict XVI, *Deus Caritas Est*, Encyclical on Christian Love, no. 6, December 25, 2005, www.vatican.va.

Chapter 18: I Am Guilty

1. Pope John Paul II, *Evangelium Vitae*, Encyclical on the Value and Inviolability of Human Life, no. 32, March 25, 1995, www.vatican.va.

Chapter 19: A Clean Refrigerator

1. Thérèse of Lisieux, *Autobiography of St. Thérèse of Lisieux*, trans. Ronald Knox (New York: P.J. Kenedy & Son, 1958), p. 237.

1. Thérèse of Lisieux, p. 266.

Chapter 21: A Catholic Warrior

1. Joseph Ratzinger, *God and the World: A Conversation with Peter Seewald* (San Francisco: Ignatius, 2002), pp. 457–458.

Chapter 22: The Christmas Spirits

1. Pontifical Council for Justice and Peace, *Compendium of the Social*

Doctrine of the Church, no. 263, www.vatican.va. See *CCC*, #2427; John Paul II, *Laborem Exercens*, Encyclical Letter on Human Work, September 14, 1981, no. 27.

Chapter 23: A Punk Rocker Child of God

1. Pope John Paul II, homily "Truth, Justice, Peace and Faith to Construct a Better World" May 6, 1984, www.vatican.va.

Chapter 24: A Pain in the Back

1. Pope John Paul II, *Rise, Let Us Be on Our Way* (New York: Warner, 2004), p. 67.

1. Mother Teresa, as quoted in David Scott, *A Revolution of Love: The Meaning of Mother Teresa* (Chicago: Loyola, 2005), p. 54.

Chapter 25: A Hero and an Angel

1. "The works of mercy are charitable actions by which we come to the aid of our neighbor in his spiritual and bodily necessities [see Isaiah 58:6–7; Hebrews 13:3]" (*CCC*, #2447).

Chapter 27: Wrestling With God

1. The *New American Bible* and the *Revised Standard Version* Catholic Edition translate the word that I call a "representative" as "man." Some commentators identify this "man" as an angel, while others say it was the Second Person of the Trinity, the God-man, Jesus. However, it is beyond question that Jacob knew that he had wrestled with God. In Genesis 32:31 Jacob specifically says, "I have seen God face to face" (*NAB*).

2. For a New Testament example, see the story of the persistent widow in Luke 18:1–7.

Chapter 28: A Fellow Human Being

1. Pope John Paul II, *Evangelium Vitae*, no. 2, emphasis added.

2. Pope John Paul II, *Christifideles Laici*, Apostolic Exhortation on the Vocation and the Mission of the Lay Faithful in the Church and in the World, no. 64, December 30, 1988, www.vatican.va.

Chapter 29: The Best Wine

1. Dom Jean-Baptiste Chautard, *The Soul of the Apostolate* (Trappist, Ky.: Gethsemani Abbey, 1946), pp. 4–5. First sentence echoes a letter of Pope Leo XIII to Cardinal Gibbons, January 22, 1899.

Chapter 30: T-shirt Theology

1. Pope John Paul II, Homily at World Youth Day, June 29, 1999, no. 2, www.vatican.va.

ABOUT THE AUTHOR

REGIS J. FLAHERTY is director of the Gilmary Retreat Center and has over thirty years of experience in working with Catholic organizations. A best-selling author, he has also written *Last Things First; The How-To Book of Catholic Devotions: Everything You Need to Know But No One Ever Taught You* (coauthored with Mike Aquilina). Regis and his wife, Libbie, are contributing authors for *Catholic for a Reason IV: Scripture and the Mystery of Marriage and Family Life.* His articles have appeared in numerous national and diocesan publications. Regis has appeared on several radio and television programs including EWTN's *Bookmark, The Abundant Life* with Johnnette Benkovic, and *Searching the Word* with Chuck Neff. He is a frequent speaker at Catholic gatherings and directs retreats on the topic of lay spirituality. Regis is the father of four and grandfather of four.